"UNAUTHORIZED"

He is probably the most famous "doctor" in America, yet even to friends of years' standing he is a "loner."

Headlines play up his emotional explosions, his love life and his feuds, his huge income. But until now, nobody has written the whole real story of his life.

Here is the book that Vince Edwards did not want written—by the one man who could write it best.

ABOUT THE AUTHOR

Only George Carpozi, Jr. could have written this book. A prize-winning newspaperman (Assistant City Editor of the *New York Journal-American* he is the author of many feature articles for the national magazines; and as "The biographer of the stars" he has written the following books!

The Brigitte Bardot Story

Marilyn Monroe: Her Own Story

Clark Gable

Gary Cooper

Let's Twist

Vince Edwards

VINCE EDWARDS

A Biography of
Television's "Dr. Ben Casey"

by
George Carpozi, Jr.

This book is respectfully dedicated to a charming and wonderful little lady with glowing red hair, a fiery spirit to match, and a heart filled with love and pride for her son. "He doesn't want a book written about himself," she told me, "but Vince Edwards is my son and I want you to write it and let the world know about him."

To Mama Julie Zoine—the proudest mother in Brooklyn, U.S.A.

Originally published in 1962

Contents

Acknowledgments

The author is deeply indebted to Vincent Edwards' family for information and background about the subject of this biography. Most especially he wishes to thank Mrs. Julie Zoine, Vince's mother, who spent many long hours with the author in recollections about her famous son. Gratitude also must go to Vince's twin, Bob, and brother Joseph, and their wives, as well as Mrs. Nancy Albanese, Vince's sister. Without their help this book would not have been possible.

The author is further indebted to numerous editors, writers, columnists, and publications for supplementary information on the life and career of Vince Edwards.

To one and all the author expresses profound thanks. Appreciation goes out to the following:

Head Librarian Paul Feis and the Reference Department of the *New York Journal-American*; Jack Podell, editor of *Photoplay Magazine*; Claire Safran, managing editor of *TV Radio Mirror*, and Larry Thomas, editor of *Motion Picture Magazine*.

Also to these newspapers, magazines, wire services and their writers, whose contributions ranged from full-length feature articles to individual reports, dispatches, reviews, and commentary:

New York Journal-American—Jack O'Brian, Dorothy Kilgallen, Louis Sobol, Howard Colson; *New York Mirror*—Harry Altshuler, John David Griffin; *New York News*—May Okon, Kay Gardella, Ben Gross, Don Nelson; *New York Times*—Jack Gould; *New York Herald-Tribune*—Joe Hyams; *New York World Telegram & Sun*—Harriet Van Horne, William Peper; *New York Post*—Bob Williams; *Variety*—Dave Kaufman; *Newark Evening News*—Tom Mackin; *Waterbury Republican*—William Homick; B*ridgeport Herald*—Cecil Smith; *Boston Globe*—Percy Shain; *Boston Sunday Herald*—Arthur E. Fetridge; *Indianapolis Times*—Richard K. Shull, Julia Inman; *Chicago American*—Bill Irvin; *Washington Post*—Laurence Laurent; *Milwaukee Journal*—Hal Humphrey, Wade Mosby, J. D. Spiro; Milwaukee Sentinel—Charles Witbeck; *The Charlotte News*—Emery Wister; *Salt Lake City Desert News and Telegram*—Howard Pearson; *Oakland Tribune*——Bill Fiset; *San Mateo Times*—Bob Foster; *San Francisco Examiner*—Dwight Newton; *Los Angeles Herald-Examiner*—Bob Hull, Bill Kennedy, Paul Baessler; *London Sunday Pictorial*—John Edwards; *United Press International*—Doc Quigg; *Associated Press*—Bob Thomas; *TV Guide*—Gilbert Seldes; *Saturday Evening Post*—Bill Davidson; *TV Week*—Donald Freeman; *TV Scout*—Joan Crosby; *Hearst Headline Service*—Dorothy Masters, Bob Hull; and for unsigned articles in the *New Orleans Tele-Viewer*,

Santa Maria Times, *Indianapolis Star*, and *Indianapolis News.*

Also *Photoplay*—Tony Wall; *TV Radio Mirror*—Arthur Henley and Dr. Robert L. Wolk; *Motion Picture*—Marilyn Beck; *Movie Mirror*—Pat Murphy; TV and Movie Screen——Chuck Miron; *Hollywood Screen Parade*—Nancy Streebeck; *Modern Screen*—Marcia Borie, Ed DeBlasio; *Movie Stars*—Lorraine Gauguin.

To Bettye Ackerman, Sam Jaffe, Sherry Nelson go many special thanks for information they provided—at times unaware they were contributing to this biography.

To all officials at the American Broadcasting Company who opened their files to the author and contributed photographs for this book, heart-felt appreciation.

To John Pascal, Night City Editor of the *New York Journal-American*, and to Mort Young, William McFadden, and Richard Barr, all of the *Journal-American* staff, goes the author's gratitude for providing invaluable editorial assistance.

—George Carpozi Jr.

THE NIGHT THEY FRIED THE DASHER

THE SNOW whirled down relentlessly on tenement-lined Marion Street, a little slit of a block burrowed in the labyrinth of thoroughfares that crisscross Brooklyn in endless procession. It was past ten. The kids were supposed to be in bed. But there wasn't a closed eye in the whole miserable block.

Clutching their frayed jackets against their necks to keep from freezing, groups of tough-faced teenagers trudged stoically through the thickening blanket of white toward Cactus' Pool Room. This was where the neighborhood kids congregated. It was headquarters.

Most times, in Cactus', they could rub elbows with the hoods and gamblers, the guys who comprised a fraternity of the underworld always to live in infamy—Murder, Inc.

This was the East New York section which melted in with the notorious Brownsville patch of Brooklyn, the territory infested by The Mob. It was the base of operations from where the gang's dread chieftains spread their web over much of New York City's empire of crime.

February 20, 1942, was a special night. The whining snowstorm rapidly piling up drifts in the streets and doorways had no effect on the plans of the neighborhood. Everyone was determined to tune in the radio to the ten o'clock newscast for the "important bulletin" the listeners were promised.

Vinnie Zoine was not one of the kids in the bunch that went to Cactus'. He wasn't allowed out that late, as a rule. But this was an exception.

He left his apartment on Marion Street and plowed through foot-thick mounds of snow cresting the sidewalk. He wore no boots—he didn't have any. Shoes were good enough, and besides he only had to go a short distance.

Vinnie stamped his feet gingerly as he entered the cold-water flat, kicking off the snow. He traced his way through the dark hall, then laboriously climbed the narrow, creaky stairs to the second floor. The only light was the one that seeped from the crack in a partly open door.

Vinnie tapped on the door gently and then pushed it open.

"Hello," he muttered solemnly to the people gathered in the living room. The radio was tuned to the news. The commentator had just begun to report on the war developments in Europe.

A youth about Vinnie's age, about ten, rose from his chair and stalked over to the visitor.

He tugged Vinnie's arm. "Let's go downstairs," Joe said. "I don't want to be here when the guy reads the bulletin. Mom will scream her head off."

He ushered Vinnie out of the apartment and back downstairs, out into the howling snowstorm, which seemed to be getting worse. The wind snarled louder as the boys turned the corner to seek smart refuge in Cactus' Pool Room.

"I guess you feel bad, eh Joe?" Vinnie said. He shouted above the roar of the wind.

"Yeah," Joe replied, morose. "But it's the family. They're taking it real bad. Mom's been crying all day."

They trudged through the deep snow to Cactus' doorway, then stopped as suddenly as if they'd walked into a stone wall. An eerie scream was piercing the cry of the wind.

It was a woman's voice.

It was Joe's mother.

Silently, they gazed at each other, fighting back the first tears starting to shimmer in their eyes.

Suddenly, Vinnie and Joey were shaken by wild howls that seemed to rock the block. The voices pitched in such a crescendo that they all but drowned out the steady, monotonous moan of the wind.

The kids who had stayed up for this eventful night had broken out into a din of unrestrained shouting.

It was triggered by the bulletin which finally came over the air. Just a flash from thirty miles up the river at Ossining, New York. But it was delivered by two thousand volts of electricity.

The warden of Sing Sing Prison had made the announcement that all Brownsville was expecting breathlessly. Now it was being broadcast over most of New York City's radio stations.

"The word from the Death House," said one of the announcers in urgent tones, "is that two more members of Murder, Inc. have been executed in Sing Sing's electric chair.

"Warden Lewis E. Lawes had just confirmed that Dasher Abbadando and Happy Mione went to their deaths calmly, stoically, resigned to their fates. A priest was with them to the end . . ."

Vinnie and Joey hadn't listened to the broadcast. But they heard the weird shouts of reaction along the street, bursting out of the grim tenements and dank hallways where the kids had been huddled anxiously around radios.

It was all over.

No question in Vinnie's and Joey's minds.

Dasher Abbadando, Joey's father, had been fried!

More than twenty years have gone by since that winter night. Murder, Inc. is but a shivery memory now. The nightmare of World War II has long passed. The fright of Korea has ended. Even the frenzies of rock 'n' roll and the Twist are fading into obscurity after jarring civilization with all the force of a figurative atom bomb.

More than twenty years have gone by and, in retrospect, the world has survived ordeal after ordeal, crisis upon crisis.

Even now we live cheek by jowl with the threat of overnight extinction. But we roll merrily along toward our destinies, whatever they may be.

And what of Vinnie Zoine?

What ever became of him?

He might have turned out to be a gangster. He could have joined the ranks of Murder, Inc. or gone on the crooked road of crime that would have led inevitably to jail—the ultimate destination for many of his old neighborhood cronies.

Vinnie Zoine escaped the fate of jail, but he did not elude violence, terror, and the spill of blood. Today he lives in this climate of blazing dramatic intensity, and he seems perfectly compatible with his surroundings.

He is, in fact, magnificently right for it all. He is big at six feet two, burly at 210 pounds, handsome despite his broken-nosed countenance. His hair-chested all-male build can give a girl goose pimples. And his soft, gentle brown eyes reflecting the sensitivities of a poet belie his surly, sharp-tongued bark, his occasional growl, his snarl that give him the reputation that follows him everywhere he goes—the reputation of an angry young, man.

That would be the portrait of Vinnie Zoine grown up today, but Vinnie Zoine is no more.

Today his name is Vincent Edwards—the dour, dynamic, dedicated Doctor Ben Casey of far-flung television fame.

1
JULIE'S STORY
THE FAMILY OF VINCE EDWARDS

IN THE BEGINNING there was Julie Morante and Vincent Zoine and they lived in a little picture-postcard place called Benevento, in Italy, four thousand miles from Times Square, seven thousand miles from Hollywood.

Friendships often grew into warm and enduring relationships between families in Benevento, and the sadness and joys, the successes and frustrations of one were shared unequivocally by the other with compassion and zeal.

It was this way between the Morantes and Zoines, who were neighbors in the small mountain province before the tum of the century.

Julie, who was born in 1895, was the first of seven children Carmine and Angela Morante raised. When she was two, a sister, Alice, joined the family. But the happiness which should have flowered with the advent of these blessed events somehow failed to materialize fully for the parents. Poverty was the villain and they soon realized that their future in Benevento was grim and uncompromising.

Carmine and Angela heard of a great land across the sea and of the rich opportunities it offered to all who ventured to its shores.

"We don't have much money," Carmine told Angela, "but I think we can scrape enough if we sell the house to buy the passage to America."

There was sadness commingled with the anxiety of moving his family to the United States, for Carmine loved his native Italy and would never have considered leaving Benevento if he were not shackled by the frustrations that clung like barnacles to the country's middle classes in those years. Italy was an abjectly poor nation and conditions already were forcing more and more families to join the growing migration to the land of opportunity on the other side of the Atlantic.

It was in the early part of 1898 that Carmine Morante had finally sold the house and obtained the needed money to take his family on their great adventure across the sea. There was sadness and tears that flowed from the heart as the family departed. Julie, who was three, and Marie, who was one, were, of course, too young to realize what was happening.

The goodbyes were threnodies of remorse. It was most difficult saying *arrivederci* to their closest friends, the Zoines, whose families had known each other for generations. There was one special last message that Angelo Zoine had for Carmine Morante.

"If things are good in America," he said hopefully, "let me know and maybe we will come over, too."

It was a crowded ship which took the Morantes, four among hundreds of other optimistic emigrants, on the fateful voyage over the storm-whipped Atlantic, to New York in the late winter of 1898.

The Statue of Liberty . . . Ellis Island . . . A Hudson River dock on West 48th Street . . . A trolley car . . .

These were the first sights the Morantes remembered as they made their way with their luggage to their new home that friends in America had rented for them in Brooklyn.

"I remember even as a girl of three that it was a very beautiful city," Julie recalls today with a vividness that indicates the depths of first impressions on a child of three. "The streets were cobblestoned and clean, except for the droppings left by the horses. Nothing was motorized then. Henry Ford hadn't become a household word yet, and the Wright Brothers' fantastic invention was still a distant vision.

"I had thought that our Roman Catholic church in Benevento was beautiful, but I was awed by the magnificence of the churches in Brooklyn. And there were so many . . ."

Indeed Brooklyn had its churches then, and still dominates the city as "The Borough of Churches."

Papa Morante and his family found soon enough that the opportunities promised in America were not mere figments of the imagination. He got a job within seven days as a laborer on the first subway construction. It was good pay but hard work. He knew that hard work was the only way to happiness and prosperity.

The weeks spun into months and the months wove a fabric of years.

In time, Papa Morante found easier ways to make a living than pounding a pick and shovel into the stone-filled earth of New York. He was able now to read and write English. His family had grown—besides Julie and Alice they had Jack and Joe and Frank and Antoinette and Jenny. Seven children now.

So many of his neighbors in Brooklyn who had come over from Italy had found job security and guaranteed paid retirement in their old age by working for the Department of Sanitation. To Morante this was a golden opportunity.

"I am going to become a garbageman," he announced happily one day to his wife. There was no objection. It was a respectable, well-paying job, comparatively speaking, and to a recent immigrant it was the fulfillment of much that this country had promised.

"They gave my father a horse and wagon and a route that took him past our house," daughter Julie remembers fondly. "We used to stand on the stoop waiting for Dad to come by and empty the garbage cans. He used to do it all by himself. They had no helpers in those days. We were so proud the first time we saw him in his uniform."

Julie also grew to love the horse that pulled her father's garbage wagon.

"We called him Ben—short for Benevento," she recalls. "I used to snitch an apple from Joe the vegetable man and feed it to Ben every time Dad came by the house."

Papa Morante was grateful to the country that enabled him to find the happiness and security he wanted for his family. He often remembered the people he had left behind in Italy and frequently sent them gifts of clothes and food—even cash.

And he also wrote, as he had promised, to his old Benevento neighbors, the Zoines.

"America is everything you have heard it is," he wrote. "Come over and see. Anybody can work here and make money. You can raise your children to be big men if they have the desire to succeed. Sell the house. Bring the family over."

But conditions in Italy had deteriorated and the Zoines could not raise money for passage. However, they did have just enough to pay the fare of their oldest son, Vincent, and, they did not want to deny him a chance to make the most of his life. The Morantes knew Vincent; he had been like a son to them. He was seven years older than little Julie and would always be available when Mama Morante called him to take their daughter out for a ride in her carriage. He was "big brother" to Julie.

"We are sending Vincent to America," wrote Papa Zoine one day in the spring of 1906. "When he gets there, he is going to stay with his uncle who lives in your great city of New York. But I will want you to watch over him as you would your own son. I know he will need your help to find his way in a strange new country."

As Fate would have it, Vincent's new home with his uncle was a mere stone's throw from the Morantes' comfortable brownstone residence in the East New York section. Only a block separated the houses on Pleasant Place.

Julie was eleven years old on that May day of 1906 when she and her nine-year-old sister Alice stood on the stoop gazing aimlessly down the street. They were wondering where to go and play. Suddenly their attention was drawn by a tall teenaged boy who had just turned the corner. Their eyes focused on him with incredulity as they scanned the ill-fitting clothes he wore.

"He had on a pair of tight reddish-brown pants that clung to his legs like winter underwear," Julie can remember as clearly as if she were looking at him now. "He was wearing button-hook patent leather shoes that we could hear squeaking as he walked halfway down the block. There was a loud red scarf wrapped around his neck over a green turtleneck sweater. His hair was slicked down and shone in the sun as if he had used a whole jar of pomade on it. And on top of his head was the funniest looking porkpie hat."

Julie and Alice watched the young man with increasing interest as he approached, for he suddenly raised his hand and waved to them as if he knew them.

All at once Julie turned to Alice ready to burst with laughter.

"Who," she asked, barely able to contain herself, "is that clown?"

"I don't know," Alice managed to say between guffaws.

"Hello, Julie," the youth said with a shy smile as he reached the stoop. "Don't you remember me?"

Julie suddenly stopped giggling and peered at the young man's face. There was something about his blue eyes and the contour of his nose and the edge of his smiling lips that struck a note of faint recognition. She stared somewhat puzzled for a long moment, then gasped, dumb-founded, as she remembered where she had seen those features before.

"Vincent!" she shrieked.

The youth dashed up the stairs and took Julie in his arms, kissing her gently on the cheek.

"You do remember your 'big brother,' don't you?"

He turned to Alice.

"You were just a tiny baby," he said wistfully.

Alice was no longer laughing *at* the young man but laughing *with* him. It was laughter of happiness at seeing someone from "home." She didn't remember Vincent but she had heard her parents—and Julie—speak of him.

The girls took Vincent upstairs to meet their parents who greeted the visitor with open arms and misty eyes. There was a big dinner that night for the guest and afterward he told of the hardships that the folks back in Benevento had to endure.

"I will work and send them money," he said. "They need all the help they can get."

Vincent was eighteen and big and strong. "I can work at anything," he told Papa Morante. "Just find me a job like you promised my father."

That wasn't difficult to do in those years when New York was burgeoning with new construction of subways and skyscrapers. Papa Morante spoke to friends who worked on the subway excavations and they told him to send Vincent down to see them. He was hired at once as a ditch-digger and he went to work.

Over the months and years that passed Vincent continued to toil as a construction laborer, saving his money faithfully and sending what he could of it to his parents in Italy. He was frugal in his living and a homebody. Instead of going out on the town as so many other young people would do, Vincent stayed close to home. He visited the Morantes twice, sometimes three times a week.

Over those months and years, too, he watched the little girl named Julie grow up and flower into a lovely young lady. Neither he nor Julie had considered themselves seriously, for theirs, from the beginning, had been a "little sister" and "big brother" relationship. But then one day in the late fall of 1911 when he had come to the Morantes for dinner, he was sharply surprised to hear Julie's father speak about a letter he received from Vincent's father back in Benevento.

9

"He is asking," Papa Morante said with a smile, "when you and Julie will be married. Your father has already picked Julie for his daughter-in-law . . ."

Vincent and Julie looked at each other in utter embarrassment, the blood rushing to their faces.

"I agree," intruded Papa Morante on the children's period of silent deliberation forced by the impact of his boldness. "I think you would make a wonderful couple."

Julie was only sixteen, Vincent twenty-three. They had no thought of marriage to each other. For that matter, they had not even thought of marriage to anyone. But now they could think about it—and did.

Vincent asked Julie for their first date.

"He took me to Coney Island swimming," Julie recalls. "He was very shy when he saw me come out of the bathing house in my full-length bathing suit. He hardly looked at me during the whole afternoon."

But Vincent must have seen enough of Julie in, her bathing suit to maintain interest. He dated her again, then again, and again.

On Christmas Eve, when Vincent came over to visit the Morantes, he took Julie by the hand and led her off to a corner of the living room next to the gaily decorated tree. He put his hand in his pocket, pulled out a small box, and opened it.

The reflection from the box caught Julie's eye immediately. She stared at it for a long moment, fascinated and surprised.

"Will you marry me?" Vincent whispered, taking a handsome diamond ring from the box.

"Yes, yes," Julie cried eagerly.

Vincent took Julie's left hand into his and slipped the ring over the third finger. And while her mother and father and sisters and brothers watched with delight on their faces, Vincent drew Julie tenderly into his arms and kissed her.

They set the wedding date immediately—it would be the following month.

"I must write to your father at once," Papa Morante said. "This will be the Christmas present from me to him."

On January 28, 1912, Vincent and Julie walked down the aisle of Lady of Loretto Roman Catholic Church at the corner of Sackman and Pacific Streets in Brooklyn and became man and wife in the eyes of God.

It was a big wedding and the church, big as it was, was crowded with the relatives and many friends of both families. The wedding reception that followed at the Morantes' house lasted until dawn.

"Nobody could beat the Italians in those days when it came to a wedding," Julie Zoine smiles today looking back on that happy, peaceful period of world history which was also the beginning of a long and happy marriage for her.

"You can say," Mrs. Zoine says, "that ours, in a way, was a mail-order marriage. But it was ordered from a catalogue printed in heaven.

"I was never happier in my life than when I became Mrs. Vincent Zoine—bride."

Julie and Vincent Zoine didn't have to go apartment or house-hunting after they were married; Papa and Mama Morante opened the doors of their comfortable and spacious flat on Pleasant Place to the newlyweds and gave them a bedroom of their own.

It was a good life from the beginning.

"We were a big, loving Italian family," Mrs. Zoine recalls. "I was home all day with my mother, helping her with the house-cleaning and the cooking, while my father and Vincent were away at work. When they came home at night we'd have the table all set and we'd sit down together in the kitchen for dinner. Afterward we'd move into the parlor and sit around talking and laughing into the night. It was homey."

Papa Morante used to carry the conversational ball, and invariably he veered to one favorite subject.

"Well," he'd say to his son-in-law, "what are you waiting for? When are you and Julie going to make me a proud grandfather?"

Julie and Vincent got used to the jibing. But it didn't go on for too long. In fact, no more than three months. It was in the month of April that Julie learned from Dr. Emanuel DeGatano that she was pregnant. Dr. DeGatano was the family physician and, conveniently for all the Morantes, lived across the street. Conveniently, too, for the newly married Zoines.

On December 16, 1912, Mrs. Zoine awakened with labor pains. Dr. DeGatano was summoned. Three hours later, he delivered Julie of a bouncing seven-pound boy.

He was named Carl.

Papa Morante had his wish.

Two years later, on August 18, 1914, the grandparents were thrilled again as they welcomed another addition to their household, a girl named Mary.

Another two years passed and on March 26, 1916, Mrs. Zoine again gave birth to another girl, Nancy.

By now, it became apparent that at the rate the Zoine family was expanding they could not possibly remain in Julie's parents' home, for it was beginning to bulge with occupants. Julie and Vincent looked for a place of their own and found a vacant apartment just down the street on Pleasant Place.

No sooner had they settled into their own home with the three children than there was another blessed event upon them—it was Helen who made her debut on April 6, 1918. Then, as if to round out the family, Mrs. Zoine gave birth to another boy, Joseph, on July 26, 1921.

"I was twenty-six and I had five children," Mrs. Zoine said. "I thought that was enough and I decided then to settle down and raise the family. I had had all I wanted to have with child-bearing."

It was a long road that Julie and Vincent had traveled from Benevento and the memories of their native Italy had faded with the years into misty and vague recollections. They were in America now, the land of opportunity. Vincent found his niche in the construction work he had first taken on in this country. He worked at it diligently and determinedly as most immigrants were prone to do. While he did not become a giant or millionaire in the construction industry, Vincent achieved a modest workman's living which was all he really wanted. He had a fine family, a lovely wife, and a fine place they called home. Most importantly, they were happy.

What more could he want?

Brooklyn, U.S.A., was a far cry from Benevento, Italy. But the family's happiness was destined for a disheartening setback. It happened in the winter following Joe's birth. Helen, the next youngest to Joe, caught a cold. Before it could be brought under control, it developed into double pneumonia. Helen died.

Helen's loss pitched Julie Zoine into the depths of depression, and might have brought on a serious emotional crisis if it hadn't been for the blessings of her other children.

"They kept me so occupied tending to their needs and wants that I was able to go on," Mrs. Zoine said. "It's pretty hard to forget a child you've lost, but when you have other youngsters around who need a mother's constant attention it helps to ease the pain in your heart."

Mrs. Zoine was a full-time mother.

"I never let them out of my sight," she explains. "I was constantly on the alert. I had to know just where they were and what they were doing. If any of them were delayed I insisted that they call me so I wouldn't worry.

"I wasn't too strict with them—just careful."

Julie Zoine's days were crammed with cleaning, cooking, and the duties of rearing four active children. Add to that "bright" children. It was Mrs. Zoine's theory that the youngsters should be brought up self-dependent and self-sustaining. A good way to start them on the right foot toward those goals, she reasoned, was to enroll them in school early.

"I got them all into kindergarten at the age of five," Mrs. Zoine said. "I believed it was good to let them learn at an early age to get along with others. I also kept after them with their studies. They never let me down. They were all bright children and their grades showed it. The result was that they all skipped classes in grammar school."

It was in September, 1927, that Mrs. Zoine first began to feel relaxed and the pressure easing off her back. By now her children were no longer the little problems they were as infants and toddlers. Joe, at six, was the youngest, Nancy was eleven, Mary, thirteen, and Carl, fifteen.

Then it happened.

"I learned I was going to have another baby," Mrs. Zoine said with a shake of her head as she recalled how utterly surprised she was to learn the news from her doctor. "I hadn't expected to have another baby, but I accepted it philosophically. It was God's will."

Husband Vincent also received the tidings with mixed emotions for he, too, had just about concluded that his family had reached its maximum limits.

"Well," he said to his wife after she bore him the greeting, "let's tell the one guy in this world who will be thrilled the most to hear you're going to have another baby—your father."

Indeed, Papa Morante was thrilled. As the months passed, Julie's father lavished attention on his daughter as never before during her pregnancies.

"He kept staring at my stomach," Mrs. Zoine chuckled, "and he kept asking me how I felt. My mother would take him to task and tell him he was getting senile in his old age. 'Leave the girl alone,' she would scold. 'This isn't going to be Julie's first baby.'

"But Papa continued to concern himself deeply with my condition, and none of us could understand why."

Papa Morante must have had a sixth sense—or some clairvoyant faculties—as time would prove. One day he revealed his hand in the unusual interest he had been displaying in Julie's ingravidation.

"You know," he smiled with an air of confidence, "I think it's going to be twins this time."

Julie looked at her father with a blank expression.

"For heaven's sake, Pop," she cried, "stop talking like that. I didn't even want one in the first place, and now you're trying to make it two!"

The weeks went by. Julie Zoine was constantly confronted by her father's reminder that she was "carrying big."

"I didn't have to be reminded," Mrs. Zoine said. "I could see what was going on just by looking down at myself. After a while others remarked that I might have twins.

"The doctor himself didn't seem fazed. He never said anything to me, nor I to him. In those days a doctor didn't do much investigative work. It never occurred to him to X-ray his patient to find out what to expect.

" 'You're doing fine, Julie,' he'd say to me. 'You'll probably be needing me sometime in October.' "

That was October of 1928 which had been set by the doctor as the target date for Mrs. Zoine to give birth.

So on July 26th of that year, when her sister Alice came over to give Julie a hand with the house, there was no thought in their minds about a sudden emergency that might arise—an emergency introduced quite unexpectedly by a sharp outcry as Julie was pressing the children's clothes.

"Alice! I'm feeling the pains . . ."

Julie Zoine had felt those same pains five times before in her lifetime.

"Quick," Julie shouted, "get Dr. DeGatano!"

As fast as she could, Alice took Julie into the bedroom and laid her down in bed. "Rest . . . don't move," she pleaded. "I'll be right back with the doctor."

It was just a matter of dashing across the street to summon the physician. In minutes, Alice was back with Dr., DeGatano, lugging his black leather physician's bag.

He took one look at Julie.

"How far apart are the pains?" he asked, leaning forward and pressing.

"Every ten seconds," Mrs. Zoine said with a grimace.

The doctor turned to Alice quickly.

"Have you got fast feet?" he asked curtly, staring past her at the door.

"Yes," Alice stammered.

"Run to the drug store," he ordered. "Bring cotton, baby oil . . ."

Mrs. Zoine doesn't remember what else the doctor asked for. All she can remember through the harrowing pain she endured in the bedroom of her home, without the comforting relief of anesthesia, without any modern devices of medicine that could be found in a hospital was that she was delivered of a red-haired boy at precisely 5:55 P.M. on that twenty-sixth day of July, 1928.

It should have been all over then, but it wasn't.

"Steady, Julie," Mrs. Zoine remembers the doctor saying.

Her next recollection is that there was more hurried, frantic efforts on the doctor's part as Alice looked away with a stunned expression from her task of washing down the baby that had just been born.

Again in those throbbing minutes that followed her first ordeal, Mrs. Zoine doesn't recall clearly exactly what happened.

"All I know is that my father was right," she says now as she looks at the magazines, newspapers, and the other publications which devote unlimited space to pictures and stories of Vincent Edwards, television's famous Dr. Ben Casey.

She points to the handsome, young man who is known to millions as the curt, caustic, rude, and bad-tempered Dr. Casey, and she says, "He's my twin son."

Indeed, Vince Edwards is Julie Zoine's beloved twin son, born in the wake of all the pain and suffering she experienced in those minutes that followed the birth of the red-haired infant at 5:55 P.M.

Vince was delivered at 6 P.M., five minutes after his twin brother. And like his twin, Vince, too, had red hair. Bright, flaming carrot-colored hair. And also like his twin, Vince weighed seven pounds on the nose.

"Call Papa," Julie whimpered beseechingly, the tears streaming down her cheeks as she gazed glassy-eyed at her two new sons. "Hurry, Alice, tell Papa. He'll be so happy."

Papa, as well as Mama Morante, were not just happy. They were exultant, as were the rest of the family—and all the neighbors for blocks around. Everyone fell in love with the twins and adored them. Most especially everyone conceded that there was hardly a difference between the two baby boys.

"They looked alike and yet there were differences that only a mother could realize," says Mrs. Zoine. "Although most people called them redheads, I could tell them apart from the shades of their hair.

"Bobby was more of a strawberry blonde, Vinnie was more auburn-haired," Julie recalls.

With twins Bobby and Vinnie, Mrs. Zoine once again had her hands tied up to the elbows in work—there were diapers to be washed, formulas to be made, not one but two infants to bathe and feed and nurse. And, to top it all, she still had four older, still-growing youngsters who needed a mother's everlasting attention.

"I didn't mind," Mrs. Zoine says today with a twinkle and bubbling pride. "It was a glorious experience and I wouldn't have traded my troubles for all the spaghetti in Italy. I was a very busy woman— but a very happy one.

"I had good children and I am proud of all of them. I am just as proud of Nancy and Joe as I am of Bobby and Vinnie. Each one has his or her own particular goodness which can only make an old lady like me today feel proud and happy that she had those children . . ."

2
THE GROWING-UP YEARS

"VINNIE WANTED the world on a string. He set out to get it right from the time we were nothing but youngsters."

There is no bitterness, no envy in Robert Zoine's voice as he speaks of his twin brother. Bob talks with pride. It is the same bubbling pride that their mother Julie exudes

when she discusses the son whom Destiny picked to climb the heights of stardom and to set off emotional bonfires as the dashing, earthy Dr. Ben Casey on thirty-two million television screens every Monday night.

Bob and Vinnie were almost identical twins during their infancy and toddlerhood. Neighbors could hardly tell them apart, except for Bob's hair which grew lighter—and curlier—while Vinnie's stayed reddish. Mama Zoine was extremely proud of Bob's curls and toiled ceaselessly to preserve them—by keeping Bob in a Buster Brown haircut until he was eight!

"You can imagine how much I liked that," Bob said. "Vinnie was lucky in that respect. He always went around with a boy's haircut. I don't think if the tables were turned, or even if Vinnie's hair was as curly as mine and Mom had tried to show off his curls to advantage, that he would have stood for it.

"That shows you how different in disposition Vinnie and I really were even in our early childhood. I was always easy-going. Vinnie was intense, demanding."

Mrs. Zoine's twin sons were good babies. She didn't detect any crankiness or unevenness in their temperaments during their early years. Neither boy was moody. Both had pleasant, smiling personalities.

"Bobby and Vinnie were such good babies that I went around recommending twins to everyone," Mrs. Zoine said proudly.

Sister Nancy, who today is Mrs. Nancy Albanese, of Brooklyn, doesn't quite go along with Mom. She has a few notions of her own about Bobby's and Vinnie's behavior as children and would like to go on record with them.

Nancy, who was twelve years old when the twins were born, should know whereof she speaks—she was the one elected to push their carriage every day.

"I didn't dub them 'the little imps' for nothing," Nancy recalls with a slight shudder. "I had my troubles with them, believe me."

Nancy's most vivid recollection of her days as nursemaid to "the little imps" harkens back to the depression years of the early 30's when the family took a thirty-dollar season locker at the Ravenhill Pool in Coney Island.

Nancy started taking Vinnie and Bob to the pool when they were five. They'd ride to the last stop on the BMT subway on a nickel—only Nancy paid. The twins were allowed to pass under the turnstiles.

Generally, Vinnie and Bob behaved on the train, but the walk to the pool was a nightmare. Nancy dreaded it because Vinnie drove her crazy. It was different than the way Vince Edwards drives the women crazy today as Dr. Ben Casey.

Nancy made a habit of buying each of the twins a frozen custard as they came out of the station. The boys would reach for their cones with all the eagerness five-year-kids can muster. But then the trouble started on the walk to the pool.

"Vinnie would gobble up his ice cream like a famished wolf," brother Bob recalls. "I was perfectly content with mine and took my time eating it. I could make it last all the way to the pool. Once Vinnie had devoured his custard, he would turn to Nancy and plead for another.

"He'd beg for a cone, or even a hot dog, at every stand we passed. Nancy couldn't contain him and almost always had to give in and buy him something else to eat."

It was that way every time Nancy took the twins to Coney. Finally, her patience gave out.

"Mom," she said one day, near tears, "I'm willing to take care of Bobby—but not Vinnie! I can't hold out against him. He's too *stubborn*. He wears me out."

Mrs. Zoine couldn't understand what Nancy was complaining about. Wasn't Vinnie always as well-behaved as Bobby?

At the pool, Nancy's troubles were multiplied as she tried to keep tabs on her little brothers romping through the crowds.

"I was deathly afraid they'd fall into the pool and drown," Nancy says. "They were the bane of the lifeguards' existence, too."

Fortunately for Nancy, the twins learned to swim almost as soon as they started their summer hiatuses to the pool. By the time they were seven, they were plowing through the deep water like a couple of tow-haired porpoises.

Their earlier days are also recalled in an anecdote told by Bob. Strangely enough, the episode is that of an accident which involved Bob and Vinnie when neither was old enough to remember himself what happened.

"We were about nine or ten months old," Bob related. "Mom had put us out into the carriage and had given Nancy the job of taking us for a stroll. Somehow or other, Vinnie and I must have gotten into a wrestling match in the carriage because all at once the carriage tipped over.

"As I understand it, we both went sprawling out of the carriage and conked our heads on the sidewalk. We howled so loud that Nancy was in panic. She began to cry hysterically. She knelt over us, examined us, saw no blood, and felt greatly relieved even though we continued to bawl our heads off.

"She put the carriage back on its wheels, lifted us into it, and went on with our stroll."

When Bob related this incident during one of my many interviews with Vince Edwards' family, Mrs. Zoine looked at her son bewildered.

"What are you saying?" she cried incredulously. I never knew this happened."

Bob smiled.

"Yeah, Mom," he said lightly. "We never told you. We didn't want Nancy to get in trouble—and we didn't want you to worry."

Bob has other memories of later years, of things that he and Vinnie did together, and how Vinnie always went for the golden ring every time.

"Vinnie showed that quality of his—the business of reaching for the moon and not giving up until he gets it—when he took his first swimming lesson," Bob recalls.

With me, it was just swimming for the fun of it. But Vinnie had to become the best swimmer in New York—candidate for the Olympics.

"He had that certain drive that never took hold of me. I guess it's the thing that's carried him right to the top as Dr. Ben Casey."

When Vinnie and Bob started kindergarten at Public School 155, at the age of five, there was little to differentiate the two. They sang as lustily as their voices allowed and messed their hands in paints as much as their teacher could stand. In deportment they were about as tame as twin wildcats.

By the time they were seven, Vinnie began to outshine Bobby in grades. The difference was a hairline. Nevertheless, it was surprising that Vinnie managed to best Bobby.

"I did my homework faithfully each day and spent long hours over it," Bob recalls. "Vinnie never split a book for class. He learned the lessons in school and read what he pleased after school."

Mrs. Zoine noticed how one son took his studies seriously while the other passed over them with a lick and a promise.

"Bobby would sit and study for hours," Mrs. Zoine said. He was a studious boy. I would have to say to him, 'Son, why don't you go outside and play?'

"Vinnie was just the opposite. I would beg him to study, but he never opened a schoolbook at home. Still and all, he'd get good marks.

"I'd say to him, 'Vinnie, why don't you study more? At least make an effort.'

"He'd smile and point his finger to his head.

"'Mom,' he'd tell me, 'I don't have to—it's all up here. When I'm in class and the teacher explains something, that's all I need.'

"Apparently he could memorize what he had to. Sort of a photographic mind."

Bob agrees with the photographic theory. "

"Vinnie didn't have to study at all," Bob said. "He was lucky that way.

"Mom stopped pleading with him to study after she saw him come home with marks as high as mine."

By the time the twins were nine, Vinnie started changing physically. He took on height and weight which in another year's time brought on a wide disparity in their appearances, removing all vestiges of the didymous nature of their births.

"Vinnie was a big eater, but I wasn't," Bob explained.

Vinnie outgrew his clothes as fast as his mother bought them.

"Soon his clothes became my hand-me-downs," Bob said.

Once he overshadowed his brother in size, Vinnie also dominated him. One windy day, coming home from school Bob was having trouble negotiating his way.

"Hey, Bob," Vinnie called. "Take my books with you. Then the wind won't blow you away."

Bob shook his head with a laugh, recalling the episode.

"I fell for it! Vinnie was always the leader—I the follower. Vinnie was aggressive and headstrong. I just went along for the ride. But together we made quite a handful for the family."

Bob recalled how he and Vinnie gave brother Joseph his share of difficulties, too.

"Mom asked Joe to take us to Hyland Park one day after school," Bob related. "We were seven and Joe was fourteen. The park wasn't far, but before we were back home Joe had felt like he'd been on a trip to the moon—walking.

"Vinnie and I thought it would be great fun to take off in different directions—to see if Joe could be in two places at the same time. I ran off and hid in the bushes, Vinnie scampered behind a tree. Joe lost us both and was running around frantically to find us.

" 'Hey, Joe!' I finally yelled. He turned and came in the direction of my voice, still unable to see me in hiding.

Then Vinnie cried, 'Hey, Joe!' from his secret place. We had Joe spinning trying to figure out where we were.

"Finally, when Joe gathered us up, he whacked us on the seats of our pants. Not hard, but just enough to sting. That asserted his authority and earned our respect for him.

"We couldn't pull the stuff we did on Nancy with Joe. Not when the guy had seven years on us—and plenty of muscle."

In school, Vinnie and Bob might have earned some recognition from their classmates for their unique position as twins. But their position was not unique. In their class alone, there were two other sets of twins—the Murphys and Smiths!

"It was funny," Bob recalls. "None of us resembled his twin too much. But we were the school's showcase classroom. Every time a visiting dignitary came to school, the principal would bring him or her to our class. He'd nod to the teacher who would then say, 'Will the Murphy and the Smith and the Zoine twins please stand up.'

"We felt like some freaks on display, but you couldn't blame the principal. After all, it wasn't every school, let alone every classroom which could boast three sets of twins."

During the growing up years, Papa and Mama Zoine had to struggle to make ends meet. The income for a laborer in those dreadful Depression years was a pittance and to keep a family of seven on a livable subsistence and adequately clothed, took a lot of stretching of every nickel. Even pennies counted heavily.

It was important, too, that every member of the family to his or her best to help in the crisis that was so characteristic of the times, affecting the overwhelming majority of Americans.

Carl, the oldest brother, was the first to contribute to the family's financial betterment. While still in high school, he got a job with a produce and liquor-distributing firm, Henry Kelly & Sons in Brooklyn. Carl gave part of his income to his parents and saved the rest. He had set an enviable goal for himself: he wanted to go to college and study medicine.

The ambition which Carl showed reflected favorably in his younger brothers, too. Vinnie and Bob, for example, had hardly cracked ten when they decided to get jobs themselves! They heard that the *Long Island Press* had after-school newspaper routes open for kids in Brooklyn.

"We went with two of our neighborhood buddies, Buster and Georgie Graziosko," recalls Bob. "The guy looked at us, puzzled, because we were on the small side. But he didn't turn us away. We got the job."

Vinnie teamed up with Buster on one route, Bob and Georgie got together on another. They tried delivering their papers on foot for a few days, then decided to become mobile.

Buster put his hands on the only available bike in the neighborhood while Georgie grabbed a beat-up coaster wagon.

"Vinnie and Buster were sure they'd get their papers delivered faster and rack up more new sales than George and I could," Bob said. "But we fooled them. George and I did much better with the wagon."

Vinnie's fortunes were better in other directions.

The neighborhood movie, the old Colonial Theatre, used to hand out tickets to the kids who could win a free admission the next Saturday if their number was posted the lobby. The winners also received a bottle of soda gratis.

"Boy, was Vinnie lucky," Bob laughed. "He won six out of seven times."

The show finally gave up the practice. No doubt the manager must have gotten a complex after seeing Vinnie hit the jackpot week after week.

But that didn't stop Vinnie from going to the movies. He patronized the show as if it were his second home. And home it was to Vinnie, too, for in those days there was not double, but triple features! Vinnie used to stay to see the show over and over—from 10 A.M. until 6 P.M.

He would have stayed longer, but there was a strict and inviolable rule that Mama and Papa Zoine had laid down for Vinnie, as well as Bob. They had to be home by six o'clock.

"We were known as the 'six o'clock babies,' " Bob says sardonically. "Most of the kids in the block could stay out until eight, but not Vinnie and me."

"That's right," Mrs. Zoine smiled. "I wanted good boys and one of the ways I knew to keep them good was to have them in the house at six. I'm glad I did it. None of my children became juvenile delinquents, and I think it was because of their upbringing. I'm proud of them all."

But Mrs. Zoine has some shuddering recollections of those bygone days, for Vinnie and Bobby on rare occasions did miss the six o'clock deadline. The chilliest episode which still haunts Mrs. Zoine is the one that occurred on the warm Sunday July night in 1942.

Vinnie and Bob, who were fourteen then, left in mid-afternoon with Buster and Georgie for a "hike." Except for the borough's parks and beaches, there is hardly any suitable terrain in Brooklyn for hiking in the true sense. No wilderness. No mountains. Just plain city streets. For Vinnie, Bob, Buster, and Georgie, all plain city kids, the streets were good enough for their hike.

When they started out, with no special goal in mind, Georgie showed his buddies four nickels—enough to bring them home on the subway if they should wander too far from home. After plodding along for what must have been miles, they decided it was time to ride back home. Already, it was six o'clock—the magic hour for the 'babies"

But lo and behold when Georgie dug into his pocket—the twenty cents had disappeared; no doubt fallen through the hole he discovered belatedly.

The boys knew they could ask a policeman to lend them fare in a pinch, but Vinnie couldn't see that.

'Why do we have to borrow money from a cop?" Vinnie said as he looked around in a strange neighborhood that neither he nor the others had ever seen before. "I know the way home. We'll walk. Follow me."

Follow Vinnie they did through one tenement-lined street after another until darkness descended in a black vail that virtually blotted out the last traces of Vinnie's graphical bearings—and his confidence.

'Let's ask a cop," he finally said, shamefaced.

The man in blue put Vinnie back on course and after another hour's hike they entered upon the familiar East New York surroundings that told the boys they were home.

Home at last—and it was 11 P.M.!

Where have you been?" screamed Mrs. Zoine, barely able contain her fury, yet obviously relieved that her twins had returned safely. She was fit to be tied. In her anxious hours of waiting with her husband, wondering what had happened to Vinnie and Bobby, Mrs. Zoine had summoned the twins' oldest sister, Mary; and Carl. Both were married now and lived away from home. They rushed over.

"When we walked in," Bob related, "Mary and Carl were sitting with Mom, trying to pacify her with assurances that we were all right, that we were old enough now to take care of ourselves."

But Mama Zoine could not be calmed. She was on the edge of hysteria, screaming that something had happened to her boys.

"Call the police, call the police!" she was crying as Vinnie and Bobby entered the living room.

After their mother had reamed them out, Vinnie and Bob were asked for an explanation. Vinnie volunteered it, telling how Georgie had lost the carfare.

"Oh, go easy with them, Mom," pleaded Mary. Carl also begged Mama to realize "the boys have got to grow up sometime."

They managed to tranquilize Mama finally—but it wasn't enough to get the twins off without punishment.

"Mom didn't allow us out of the house for a week," Bob snickered. "She was a tough baby to deal with."

That fall, Vinnie and Bob started high school. By then, Carl was working fulltime at Kelly's, supporting his wife and two children. Carl had given up the idea of becoming a doctor, after studies at Villanova University. He had gotten married, and when the children came he had to face up to the realities of life. It takes money to support a wife and young ones and he had no income at school. So Carl went back to work.

In 1945, Carl suffered a heart attack and died. He was only thirty-two.

Before Carl died, Bob had begged him to talk to the boss at Kelly's for an after-school job. Carl got Bob work as an office boy and volunteered to do the same for Vinnie.

"Nope," Vinnie said adamantly. "I don't think it'll do much good for me to work."

By now Papa Zoine was earning good money again in construction work and the family didn't have to count pennies and nickels as cautiously as in Depression days.

Vinnie had a goal in mind at last.

"I want to become an airplane mechanic," he said. I also want to concentrate on athletics."

Vinnie wasn't certain what sport he liked best, but he felt equipped for swimming and weightlifting. So he joined the YMCA and began to work out regularly in the gym and pool.

By now, too, Vinnie and Bob had begun to go their separate ways for the first time in their lives. Vinnie had a bug in his mind about flying. During his childhood he had been crazy about planes and had spent untold hours building models out of balsa and glue, stringing up the finished products all over the house. He was still going strong with his hobby. His strong interest in aviation had led

Vince to enroll in East New York Vocational High School, which offered courses in that field.

Bob was inclined toward commerce. With the promise of a good job at Kelly's, he decided to study accounting, stenography, and typing. He entered Franklin K. Lane Commercial High School, also in Brooklyn.

Separated by school, Vinnie and Bob were still together evenings and managed to do things together. Although their interests began to swing out on widely divergent paths, they continued to pal around with Buster and George Graziosko and with Bill and Eddie Devino, as well as other boys they had known since elementary and junior high school days.

But Vinnie gradually came up with a different set of friends, some from his high school, others from the Y. Yet he went on socializing with the old neighborhood chums, too, although there was less and less of it as Vinnie began to find new interests and new goals—interests and goals that ultimately brought him up from the slums of Brooklyn to television's and the entertainment world's most compelling medicine man, Dr. Ben Casey.

3
FROM BORSHT BELT TO HAWAII

IT WAS going on nine o'clock of a winter's night in 1939 and no one was home except Vinnie Zoine, who was building a model airplane with balsa wood, tissue paper and cement. Making model planes was Vinnie's favorite hobby then, while he studied aviation at East New York Vocational High School.

His twin brother Bobby returned home from a game of pool at Cactus' Pool Room and found Vinnie busy at his leisure-time occupation in the kitchen.

"It smelled to the high heavens of glue when I came in." Bob recalled it with a shrug because the memory of that night is one that will never dim in his mind.

"I remember clearly it was a Friday night. Mom had gone to the old Colonial Theatre. She used to go every Friday night because they gave away free dishes. Mom collected every dish until she completed the entire set.

"Vinnie was building a tremendous plane. It was almost as big as he was, and when he was eleven years old he was pretty big. He had just finished cementing the tissue on the skeleton of the plane and had wet it down with water to stretch the 'skin.' I

41

sat down and watched him interestedly because he was always a source of amazement to me. I couldn't understand how anybody could have so much patience with so much of the detail that went into building those planes.

"I didn't say a word, but Vinnie turned to me and said, 'Bobby, I've discovered a new way to dry the paper, Watch this . . .'

"He went to the kitchen stove and lit all four gas jets full blast. I could feel the heat of the flames over by my hair."

Bob remembers Vinnie picked up the plane, brought it the stove, and held it over the torchlike flames.

"He was holding the plane by the tail with the wings spread-eagled over the entire stove. I saw that he was holding it too close to the flames and I decided to warn him.

" 'Vinnie,' I called, 'don't hold it so near the fire.'

"He turned and snickered at me. 'What's the matter, you think I'm stupid or something.'

"Hardly had the words left his mouth than there was a sudden flash. Flames swirled up over the kitchen stove. The plane was gone in one gulp. Vinnie had barely enough time to let go of it. He jumped back with a look of astonishment on his face. He couldn't believe it happened."

The flames leaped along the wall and set fire to the pretty white lace curtains that Mrs. Zoine had hung that very afternoon. They were devoured as swiftly as the balsa and paper model plane.

"We rushed to the kitchen sink, filled pots with water, and splashed the curtains and the clean new shade, both burning furiously. Thank God we put out the fire before it could spread."

They had barely doused the great conflagration than there was the click of a key in the door.

"It was Mom, returning from the movies," Bob said. "I'll never forget that expression as she walked in. Neither will Vinnie. Mom was holding the dish she had gotten at the show. It was the only dish she was ever to break. It just fell out of her hands as she looked in horror at the curls of smoke still rising from her curtains which had been incinerated."

Vinnie and Bob don't recall what their mother had shouted, but they will never forget how loud her voice came through—even as they sought refuge under the bed.

This was part of growing up for Vince Edwards, or Vinnie Zoine as he was known in those days. Growing up where Vinnie lived was not an easy, uncomplicated task. There were many trappings, many ambuscades that implanted themselves firmly in Vince's pathway of youth.

For example, the East New York section of Brooklyn had changed in character and mood over the years since Vinnie's parents first settled there. Their neighborhood for the most part had deteriorated considerably and became overrun with young toughs, punks, and hoodlums. The once clean, ornate stone-and-brick-front houses became dilapidated eyesores.

The Zoines eventually moved from their second-floor apartment on Pleasant Place to more commodious and up-to-date surroundings on nearby Marion Street. They occupied the ground floor of the three-story private apartment building which had an imposing look about it because of a large iron fence and gate in front.

The occupant on the second floor was Dr. Harry Rosenthal, who maintained both his home and office the there.

"Mom told us when we moved in that the doctor did not want noise," Bob explained. "He didn't mind kids, so long as they were quiet. So Mom warned us to make ourselves scarce, especially during Dr. Rosenthal's office hours.

"We used to spend a lot of time on the stoop, moping mostly. Mom told us to be polite to the doctor's patients. She instructed us to open the door for them when they walked in or out of the house. The way things turned out, Vinnie and I became doormen for the doctor. Every few minutes we'd have to hop up and open the door for a patient either coming or going. We got so tired of this that we finally gave up sitting on the stoop."

An alternative hangout for Vinnie and Bobby was Cactus' Pool Room, which was a combination of three bowling lanes and billiard and snooker tables. It was only a few blocks from home. There the twins met a new set of friends from the other side of the railroad tracks, in a manner of speaking.

"Some of the kids," according to Vince Edwards, who has more vivid recollections of them than Bobby, "were pretty tough. Their fathers were rugged characters mostly. A couple, like Dasher Abbadando and Happy Mione, who lived in our neighborhood, were feared and fearless. They were members of Murder, Inc., which was a dread name in those days."

Incongruously, while Abbadando and Mione were probably as cold-blooded and terrifying as any of the mob could be, their families were warm, pleasant folks with kindness and gentleness in their hearts. They were no different than many of the fine Italian families who, with the Jewish residents, formed the dominant ethnic groups in the East New York and adjoining Brownsville sections of Brooklyn.

"Maybe they were killers," says Mrs. Zoine, looking back. "But it didn't seem to me those men had murder in their hearts. So far as I'm concerned, they never did us any harm."

In fact, if it wasn't for Happy Mione, who knows but what might have happened to Mrs. Zoine and to her daughters, Nancy and Mary, in those days.

"I was coming home late one night from visiting friends," Mrs. Zoine related with palpable tremors as she thought back on an incident involving herself. "The street was deathly quiet. Suddenly, as I turned the corner of Marion Street and approached the house, I heard footsteps behind me. Without turning, I hastened my pace.

The footsteps got faster, staying right with me. I was terrified.

"When I reached the house, I ran up the steps, opened the door, and almost pushed my finger through the bell as I rung it in panic."

In panic because Mrs. Zoine saw through the glass door the shadow of a huge man silhouetted against the white curtain. Mrs. Zoine was trapped in the vestibule

because the inner door was locked. There were only three ways it could be opened—by pressing a buzzer from the apartment, by someone from the inside, or with a key from outside. Mrs. Zoine was so gripped by irrational terror she couldn't think of opening her bag and taking out her key.

Her incessant ringing of the bell brought her husband charging out. He opened the inside door and demanded, "What's happening?"

Julie pointed to the shadow which at that moment moved away swiftly. Whoever it was had heard the man's voice and was frightened into flight.

Vincent Zoine opened the door and pursued a tall, husky figure whom he recognized as a dark man even in the shadows of the night. But the prowler ran off before Zoine could catch up with him.

The next night, Nancy and Mary came home from a church dance and encountered the same stranger who followed them home. Like their mother, they were terrified.

In the morning, Mrs. Zoine went to the neighborhood police precinct and spoke to the desk officer about the prowler.

"He listened to me as if he were bored," Mrs. Zoine related. "Then he told me, 'You can get rid of him if you take your daughters' dancing shoes away from them.'

"I was furious. He was telling me not to let my daughters out at night. I asked him what protection he could give me. He said the police were doing their best to keep the streets safe and the best I could do is hope."

None of that for Mrs. Zoine. Her irritability over the situation grew into boiling fury.

"I went over to Mr. Mione's house," Mrs. Zoine said. "I told him what had happened.

" 'Mrs. Zoine,' he said to me. 'You have nothing to worry about. That prowler will never bother you again."

"I don't know what methods Mr. Mione employed, but they certainly were effective. That prowler never bothered any of us again."

A few years later, in 1942, Mrs. Zoine was petrified when she learned that the "nice Mr. Moine" was mixed up in gangland murder, a crime for which he paid with his life along with Dasher Abbadando in Sing Sing's electric chair.

Most of the kids that lived in the East New York Brownsville sections grew up into respectable, decent citizens. But it was touch and go as to which would veer on the straight and narrow and which would strike out for a life of crime.

"Some of the kids I grew up with," says Vince Edwards, "ended up with very fancy addresses, like Sing Sing, Dannemora, and Alcatraz. It was rough growing up in my neighborhood. You didn't know from one minute to the next when you'd do something that would lead to jail, Often you'd be on the borderline of law and decency and wondering when you'd be stepping off into the quicksand of crime."

For example, the day began and ended on the streets for most of the kids. Many belonged to gangs. Many were fighting gangs, battling one another for neighborhood supremacy. Some of the kids stole hub caps and slashed tires. Others stole cars for joy rides.

"I didn't run with the street packs," Vince avers. "I had my own friends who didn't belong to gangs. But if I came up against any of the toughs, I knew how to handle myself. I didn't win all the fights—but I never ran away from any."

While other kids stole hub caps, Vinnie "fixed" them—with stones.

"It was good clean fun," says Bob as he remembers those days. "Vinnie and I had a pal named Louis Napolitano. Louis and Vinnie were the comics in our bunch.

He and Vinnie vied for the biggest laughs.

"One day Vinnie pried the hub cap off a car, put pebbles inside it, and replaced it on the wheel. The owner came out later, started the car, and drove it down the block. He wasn't halfway to the corner before he stopped, got out, raised the hood, and started looking for the knock in his motor. He was just the first of many drivers who went crazy trying to figure out the noise in their engines."

When their buddy Louis married, his bride suddenly found herself involuntarily sharing her apartment with the Zoine twins and other members of their bunch.

Louis reserved one room for "the boys" and put a sign on the door. He never knew how many would turn up for meals—or for a night's sleep.

One night the boys gathered at Louis' to listen to recorded classical music. Vinnie was the only one who didn't show up. No one had any idea why Vinnie had failed to come. Louis put on *A Night on Bald Mountain*, an eerie piece. The lights had been dimmed to set the mood.

Suddenly, while the fellows were sitting around listening to the record, there was a scratching sound on the window followed by the sudden rolling up of the shade. Everyone turned with a start, alarmed. What they saw struck such terror in the boys that half of them wheeled around screaming, burst out the door, and fled to the street. The ones who stayed behind did so only because they knew better.

"What they saw," Vince Edwards' twin Bob explained, was a youthful face dripping blood and wearing a gleaming aluminum pot on his head like some creature from outer space. To make it more grisly, the figure in the window shone a bright light on his face, which was distorted into a terrifying grimace."

The "blood" was ketchup.

The face belonged to Vinnie Zoine.

"That's my twin brother," Bob laughed. He was always the actor, even in those days. Vinnie was acting all the time, perhaps even unconsciously. I remember how he'd go at it every Halloween. Most of the kids would throw an old sack or a raggedy coat over themselves, put on a mask, and go out to raise hell. But not Vinnie. He had to make himself up like Boris Karloff, with lipstick, mascara, rouge, powder—the works. He worked at it for hours.

"Although he never expressed a desire for acting in those days, I think Vinnie had it in his blood even then. Only it didn't boil up until a few years later."

The time of the prank that Bob was talking about was 1945. Vinnie—and Bob—were seventeen then. Both Vinnie and Bob had graduated their respective high schools by now—actually they received their diplomas at fifteen—and Bob had taken the job at Henry Kelly & Sons, where brother Carl worked before he died.

Bob tried to talk Vinnie into taking a job there. But Vinnie held out against it with a deaf ear.

"But you wanted to be an airplane mechanic, and you studied the trade in school," Bob said scornfully. "What's happened?"

"I've changed my mind," pouted Vince. "I don't think you can get anywhere in this world doing manual labor."

The two years since high school graduation had brought a different outlook on life to Vinnie Zoine. He had not yet begun to envision his future in the bright, glowing, spectacular terms of his present preeminence as the celebrated Dr. Ben Casey. Nor was he even contemplating the world of acting. Television was only a distant vision in the experimental laboratory.

The year was 1944. Vinnie and Bob both graduated their respective high schools at the age of fifteen-actually they were a month away from their sixteenth birthdays.

"I was so proud of my boys," Julie Zoine said. "They were two years younger than many of their classmates. I know that my efforts to make them good boys had paid off. But the question was: what will they do now? I certainly wanted them both to go to college. But college costs money. And we didn't have it."

With all her heart, Julie Zoine wanted one of her sons to be a doctor. One of her sons started college with that lofty goal in his sights. But Carl was forced to quit college. Then death took him and the dream was dead, too. He left a widow and two young children.

For Vince, the end of high school was merely the curtain coming down on the first act in the drama of his life. Curiously, the plot for the second act had not yet been written—and there Vince was in the wings, waiting to come on stage.

What could he do?

"I'm not really sure what I want," he told his mother that late spring following graduation. "I think that I'll try for a job at the beach. Maybe they'll take me on as a lifeguard." Vince still was only a legal fifteen. An applicant for a lifeguard's position must be sixteen. And a good, resourceful swimmer. Vince was good and resourceful as a swimmer. He had been on the high school team and shown his mettle by winning a raft of medals in inter-scholastic meets. The backstroke was his specialty.

At fifteen Vince had achieved great physical growth.

"I must have weighed 175 pounds," Vince recalls. "I was beginning to have muscles on my muscles. I had tried my hand at every sport—stickball, touch football, just about everything we could play on the street. And I also did a lot of swimming."

Vince, Bob said, was a whiz at touch football. He could throw the pigskin the distance of two sewers—the mark of a 50-yard passer. In stickball he could wallop the "Spaldeen" three manholes—equal to a 300-foot drive in Yankee Stadium.

And at the Y Vinnie was taking to the weights which, more than any other form of athletic activity, were adding those layers of muscles to his arms, chest, and legs.

That summer of 1944, Vince went to the Department of Parks and applied for the lifeguard's job he wanted. Vince had no trouble with the application. In the box which asked for his age, he wrote in "sixteen." It was a little white lie but it was his passport to the swimming test at Coney Island. He passed with flying colors. A week later he was notified he was on the payroll, and was ordered to report for duty at Coney.

So, here he was now—a lifeguard at the world's most populous beach. On a hot summer Sunday at Coney, the turnout generally hits two million or more. And there was Vince, a speck on the sand—but doing what he wanted most of all.

It was at Coney that summer when Vince met a fellow lifeguard named Seymour Schlanger, a champion swimmer from the Flatbush Boys Club in Brooklyn.

54

"Vinnie," Schlanger said one day after watching the enormous strength of the youthful Vince in the choppy Atlantic, "why don't you join the Flatbush Boys' Club, too?"

He took up Schlanger's invitation and, after the summer season ended at Coney, Vince signed up with the club. Vinnie was good enough to make the club's first team on his first tryout, and he became its backstroke star. He won meet after meet.

But at home, Mama Julie Zoine watched Vinnie with dismay. Bob had gotten a job and was earning a living. Vinnie still hadn't earned a red cent—unless you count the pennies he made for the brief time he worked as a newspaper delivery boy at ten.

Fall and winter of 1944 came and went and it was spring of 1945. Vince looked forward again to a summer as a lifeguard. But this time instead of Coney Island, Vince took a job at the Cypress Pool, which was near his home.

Summer passed, fall came, then winter.

It was 1946 now.

Mama Julie took Vince into the living room one day to talk with him. It was a special occasion—not the talking, but the visit to the living room. For an explanation, let Bob tell that story.

"Mom had the house divided," Bob relates. "There was the part that we lived in and the part that was set aside as a showplace. None of the kids could use that part. Let me see, there was the living room, the dining room, and Mom's and Pop's bedroom which were all forbidden territory. We had a long hall leading to that part of the house. Mom always kept all three doors locked. Actually locked.

"If anyone wanted to go into that part of the house, it was necessary to get three keys. And guess who had the keys? Mom did!

"We used to call her 'Keeper of the Keys.' "

Mrs. Zoine was listening intently when Bob told me this story. Mama Julie blushed first, then broke into a hearty laughter. I looked at her.

"Is it true, Mama Julie?" I asked.

"Oh," she said, still giggling. "If you listen to these kids of mine they'll distort anything. Don't pay any attention to what they say." And she went on laughing—almost, an admission of innocent culpableness.

When his mother brought Vinnie into the "inner sanctum," as Bob labeled the part of the house that was "locked up," she looked at her son with sorrowful eyes.

"What are you going to do with yourself?" she asked leadingly, almost demandingly, for she was approaching exasperation with her son's idleness.

Vinnie leaped to his feet, jogged across the room to his mother who was sitting in the easy chair, and gently flopped his big full-grown, six-foot frame in her lap. He kissed her sweetly on the cheek.

"Mom," he said tenderly, "I'm going to college and make something of myself."

Misty-eyed, Mrs. Zoine looked at her son with bewilderment.

"College?" she sighed as if the word were from a foreign dialect.

"Yes, Mom," laughed Vinnie, "I'm going to get an education."

"With what?" Mrs. Zoine persisted. "You don't have the price of admission to the Colonial Theatre. How will you get the money for college?"

"Easy, Mom," Vinnie said, chucking his mother under the chin. "I'm going on a scholarship."

His mother stared at Vinnie unblinkingly for a few seconds. Then a sympathetic expression coursed over her face. She shook her head sadly.

"But Vinnie," she whispered. "You were good in your grades in school—but not that good. How do you expect to go to college on a scholarship?"

"I'll get a swimming scholarship," Vinnie replied matter-of-factly. "And if Bob had any sense, he'd do the same."

Bob was listening at the door. He didn't come into the living room because Mama hadn't asked him.

"What for?" he snapped. "I've got a good job at Kelly's. What do I need college for?"

Case closed.

Mrs. Zoine threw up her hands. If Vinnie thought he could get a scholarship to college, that was all right with her. But being from Benevento was the same as being from Missouri. Vinnie had to show her.

And around the house the only thing that Vinnie showed Mama was muscle. Oh, what muscle! Vinnie at this point had taken up weight-lifting in earnest.

"My kitchen was like a gymnasium," Mrs. Zoine said. "Bell bars and weights were strewn over the floor like they were part of the equipment. I'd have to climb over them every time I went to cook or wash the dishes. Vinnie was always lifting those weights.

"I used to sit and watch him—and I'd admire his strength. Vinnie always had a good build, but the weights expanded his dimensions greatly. I finally told him one day with all the pride a mother can muster, 'Vinnie, you have a beautiful body.'

"He laughed and said, 'Aw, cut it out, Mom. You're making me blush.' "

Simultaneously with his development into a youth with a Herculean torso, Vince became a connoisseur of health and diet foods which were more than just a fad with him. You might say it was a religion. Somewhere along the line, Vince had read that organic foods were best for human consumption. These are foods that are grown without the aid of fertilizers and chemicals.

"Suddenly," Mrs. Zoine said, "Vinnie spurned my home cooking. All through the years he used to rave about the meals he had at home. Then out of the blue he tells me he can't eat my cooking."

Mrs. Zoine questioned Vinnie. He told her about organic foods. They had to be purchased in special health food stores. He would go shopping for them himself. But one day he asked his mother to pick up an item from the local grocery.

"Mom," he told her. "When you go down to Mr. Wolin's store, buy a box of wheat germ, please."

"Wheat germ?" gagged Mrs. Zoine. "Since when does germ come in boxes?"

"Please, Mom, ask for it," Vinnie pleaded.

"I will not," Mrs. Zoine said bluntly.

Later that afternoon, Vinnie came home and saw a box of wheat germ on the kitchen table.

"What happened?" Vinnie asked. "I thought you weren't going to get it."

Mrs. Zoine looked at Vinnie, and shrugged.

"If you're crazy enough to eat it, I'm crazy enough to buy it. Besides, I'm crazy about my crazy son."

In 1946, Vinnie Zoine, barely eighteen, realized a dream. He entered the Metropolitan Amateur Athletic Union swimming championships and came up against the

New York City area's toughest competition. Vinnie was honed perfectly for this moment of truth.

The starter's gun went off. Vinnie and eight competitors dove into the pool for the 100-meter backstroke event. Vinnie plowed through the water in the lead—a lead he never relinquished.

Vinnie won!

Vinnie was the Metropolitan AAU backstroke champ!

With that championship in his hip pocket, Vinnie was ready to reach for the college education he never could have afforded otherwise. His good friend, Seymour Schlanger, had already won an athletic scholarship to Ohio State University the previous year. When Vince won the championship, Schlanger put the bug in the coach's ear to get the hulking Brooklynite into the Big Ten school. That summer the dazzling prospect of a college scholarship was dangled before the eager Vinnie Zoine. He leaped at the opportunity.

Fall of 1946 came and Vinnie Zoine entered Ohio State University as a freshman. He chose business administration as his major. Actually, when Vinnie had graduated from East New York a vocational high school, he was not properly, qualified for college entrance. But he had the foresight to take night courses which gave him the necessary credits when he was accepted at Ohio State.

At college, Vince made the grade in all his courses and passed his freshman year with a B average. As an athlete, he lived up to expectations by placing fourth in the Big Ten and National Collegiate Athletic Association championships and an impressive sixth in the National AAU championships.

When he returned home for the summer vacation in 1947, swimming was still Vinnie's life. He decided that he would be a lifeguard again, which would enable him to continue training—and earn money at the same time. While in school, Vinnie had worked as a busboy in the cafeteria to make the money he needed for extras. Moreover, as a college student, Vinnie needed better clothes.

He had begun to set higher goals for himself, too, but those he could never clearly define.

His twin, Bob, sensed the change that a year in college had made in Vinnie.

"He started going with different friends and always dressed up for an appointment. I never knew where he went. If I'd ask, he'd say to me, 'You can't pal around with small people all your life or you'll never get to be big. Sometimes you have to go where the big people are.'

"He was still impulsive and you never knew what to expect next. I was the one who always thought things over carefully. Even though we were close, this difference made us seem miles apart."

Vinnie was reaching for the big people. And that summer he got to meet them. He got a job as a lifeguard at the Olympic Hotel in Fallsburgh, up in the Catskill Mountain area's well-known "borsht belt."

But the big people he met were not in the swimming pool. They were the touring entertainers— stars like Milton Berle and Myron Cohen and Buddy Hackett and Eddie Fisher. Vince got to meet them when he was called upon to help out in the nightly entertainment programs in which the stars were featured.

In the beginning, he was only a stagehand, a mover of scenery. Then the hotel owner, Mrs.

Harriet Rosenburg, who had hired Vince as a life-guard, noticed something about the strapping young man when he was backstage.

"He was such a gay young fellow—a real hit with the girls, and always clowning around. He wanted to take part in our theatrical activities. He sang, mimicked, and danced. A real jack-of-all-trades type, with a wonderful, endearing smile. One of the best-looking boys we ever had around here."

So Vinnie Zoine was asked if he would take part in the shows—on stage. He didn't have to be asked twice. For the remaining weeks of that 1947 summer season, Vinnie did about all one could expect a rank amateur to do among the professionals of the stage and screen, appearing at the hotel to entertain the guests. He sang, danced, pinch-hit as master of ceremonies, and also—probably most often—served as a stooge for the comedians.

"Frankly," says Mrs. Rosenburg in looking back, "I can hardly believe it's the same fellow, the great Vince Edwards who is television's Dr. Ben Casey—because he is so serious on TV."

Vince liked the part he got in the hotel's entertainment activities. It was an opportunity to get close to and talk to the big show business people like Berle and Hackett and Cohen.

In talking with them, and others, Vinnie also learned to turn a rather glib tongue in the Yiddish language, which helped his repertoire up in the "borsht circuit."

It was that summer when Vincent Edwards—or Vinnie Zoine as he still was known then—decided the world of acting was the world he wanted to conquer.

"The acting bug," Vince says, "bit me badly. I knew after that stay in the Catskills that I wanted to make my career in the entertainment world. But I wasn't certain of exactly what I wanted to do. I even gave thought to writing scripts—I would have done anything to stay in that business."

Thus bitten, Vince went back to Ohio State that fall as a sophomore and promptly switched from a business major to English.

"I thought that if I was going to go into show business, English would be the most important subject," Vince explained.

Back at school, Vinnie Zoine continued to star as a swimmer. This was the sport which had enabled him to go to college and the sport he still loved best. But the idea of acting constantly gnawed at Vinnie now. So he took courses in dramatics also.

But swimming was still his greatest interest and, in that year of 1948, Vince had set another goal for himself—to become a member of the United States Olympic team. With that ambition burning inside him, Vince turned his eyes toward Hawaii. Outside his dormitory in Columbus Ohio, the snow swirled down in a raging winter storm.

"How can a guy train for the Olympic team in this weather?" Vinnie asked himself. "A guy can train in the indoor pool, but it's not Olympic-sized and it isn't the same as swimming outdoors."

Where can a guy train properly to qualify for the United States swimming team?

In Hawaii, of course.

So Vince decided to transfer to the University of Hawaii. He wrote to the school and received an answer promptly. He was accepted. The school's world-famous swimming coach, Soichi Sakamoto, arranged things for Vince. He wanted this promising athlete on his team.

Vince packed his bags and flew off at once to Honolulu where the sun shines year-round and the outdoor pools are splashing with budding Olympic prospects in year-round training.

"This is for me," Vinnie Zoine smiled happily as he set foot on the beautiful and romantic mid-Pacific paradise.

It was a long way from Benevento where his parents were born, and it was still a long way from Brooklyn where Vinnie was born. But this was it. This was his life now.

"This is the greatest thing that ever happened to me."

4
THE AMERICAN ACADEMY OF DRAMATIC ARTS

THE HAWAIIAN ISLANDS are a tranquil, picturesque group of volcanic land masses shaped by nature during one of her angry moods millions of years ago. The earth was still young then. Television and Dr. Ben Casey were as far away as Venus.

The earth had aged considerably since those prehistoric times, by the year of 1948. Television was no longer a distant dream but a reality and the biggest thing on TV that year in the United States was Milton Berle. Vinnie Zoine had met him the previous summer up in New York's Catskill Mountains.

Dr. Ben Casey, of course, was unheard of, for no one in those days knew just what course television would take and how widespread it would become as an entertainment medium.

At the University of Hawaii, Vinnie Zoine had no forethought of ever achieving the greatness and adulation that belongs to him today as television's most famous man of medicine. His ambition was to make the Olympic team. But he had also begun to think in terms of a secondary goal—acting.

More and more, Vinnie thought about a career on the stage or before the cameras of Hollywood. Throughout his young life, he had had few real ambitions, other than to be a champion swimmer and to bring glory to the United States in the Olympics. Yet, after that previous summer in the Catskills, as Vince Edwards says now, he had been "bitten by the acting bug." He had tasted show business at the Olympic Hotel. He liked it.

At Ohio State, he began taking courses in dramatics, further arousing his interest in acting.

Now, at the University of Hawaii, Vince turned a keen eye to the school's dramatic club—The University of Hawaii Players—and the Honolulu Community Theatre, where the players performed. As a student of drama he was entitled to join the club, and did.

Suddenly, Vince found himself spending less and less time in the pool and more and more time with the club. His roles were secondary, but he received a great deal of encouragement from the other players as well as his drama coach.

Little by little, Vinnie began to find himself strung between twin ambitions. On the one side he had his athletic life to lead; he was the only occidental on the team, yet he was coach Sakamoto's protege. Vinnie promised a great deal as a swimmer. On the other side, there was Vinnie's acting life. He was in a quandary. One career had to yield. If he were to concentrate on dramatics, he could not give swimming the attention it required. Training for an Olympic team is a full-time job.

Then, all at once, Fate helped Vince decide. One day, he dove into the pool. A sharp, excruciating pain jabbed his right side below the abdomen. Vince struggled desperately toward the ladder. He climbed out of the water, doubled over in throbbing pain.

"I think it's cramps," Vinnie told the team doctor.

The doctor pressed his hand deeply into Vinnie's lower abdomen. Vinnie winced and let out an agonized cry.

The doctor shook his head.

"Son, you have appendicitis," he said solemnly. "I advise you not to go in the water again."

The attack was not serious enough to warrant surgery, but it doomed Vinnie's ambitions to train for the Olympic team. He was out of the running now.

That made up Vinnie Zoine's mind. He would concentrate full blast on an acting career now. His ambitions to be a swimmer and an actor had not helped his academic average at the University of Hawaii. He saw no future in school at this point.

In the middle of the semester, Vinnie packed and caught the next plane for home. Abruptly, his education was over.

"Vinnie!" squealed Mama Julie with mingled surprise and joy when she opened the door and saw her big boy standing there.

"I quit school, Mom," Vinnie said bluntly. He saw the hurt look in his mother's eyes.

"Don't worry, Mom," he went on, quickly and surely, "I'm going to be an actor."

Mrs. Zoine gazed at her son with utter disbelief.

"Are you out of your mind?" Mama Julie bellowed. "What kind of foolishness is that? Is this why I raised you—to starve all your life?"

Vinnie took his mother in his arms, kissed her tenderly on the cheek, and gently patted her still red hair.

"You'll see, Mom. I'll become an actor. You'll be proud of me someday. Just wait . . ."

The days and weeks passed swiftly. One day Vinnie came home from job hunting as he'd been doing every day since he returned from Hawaii. He was extremely depressed.

"I don't think I can get work as an actor unless I go to dramatic school," Vinnie admitted to his mother, sadly.

"Why don't you go?" she asked him without thought to the fact that schooling costs a lot of money.

Vinnie explained it in the simplest language he knew. He said, "No dough."

Then Vinnie told his mother that people said he had a good voice and that maybe he could become a singer.

"Well, son, why don't you try that?" Mrs. Zoine suggested.

"No dough," Vince repeated.

"How much will it cost?" Mama Julie inquired.

Vince said a couple of hundred dollars might do it.

"I have the money," Mrs. Zoine said. "I'll give it to you."

Vince's eyes misted.

"Mom," he said wistfully, "Mom, you're the greatest."

Vinnie took voice lessons at a private school in Manhattan. But his progress was slow, tedious, un-rewarding. He struggled through school until one day he was told that his voice would improve greatly—if he had his tonsils removed.

Vince entered New York Hospital and had them taken out. But he still got nowhere. No singing jobs were open to him. Discouragement crept over Vinnie.

One day Mrs. Zoine saw her son in one of his increasingly frequent depressions.

"What's the matter, Vinnie?" she asked.

"It's no use, Mom," he said. "I've got to go to actor's school—it's my only chance to make it in show business. I got to have training."

Mrs. Zoine studied her son's sad face.

"You know, Vinnie," she said bluntly, "I think you ought to see a psychiatrist. First you want to be an actor. Then you decide on a singing career. Now you want to be an actor again. You can't go through life hopscotching from one thing to another. You've got to make up your mind."

Vinnie looked at his mother in silence. He couldn't argue with her. She was right.

"Okay, Mom," Vinnie said. "I'll get a job."

"Now you're talking sense," Mama Julie said. "What kind of work?"

"Oh, I don't know. Maybe digging ditches."

Mrs. Zoine threw up her hands in exasperation. "After all that college training?" she asked incredulously.

"Yep," Vinnie cracked. "Strong back, weak mind, Ma."

The next day Vinnie came home dragging his heels.

"What did you do today, son?" Mrs. Zoine asked.

"Worked," Vinnie replied. "I got a job on the subway construction in Queens. I'm great with a pick."

"Son," Mama Julie said to Vinnie with the sympathy and understanding that only a mother can have for her boy. "Where would you study acting?"

"The American Academy of Dramatic Arts," Vinnie replied quickly. "It's next to Carnegie Hall on Fifty-Seventh -Street."

Nothing more was said except that Vinnie mentioned the dean's name. He brought the name up in telling his mother that the man thought Vinnie had a chance to make the grade as an actor.

"I was truly concerned about Vinnie," Mrs. Zoine told me in relating this chapter of her son's life. "After all, I didn't know what to think. He was going from one thing to another. And everything was expensive. I knew it took a great deal of training to become an actor—but I didn't know much about it. Vinnie told me it would cost eight hundred dollars for a course at the Academy. That was a lot of money, especially for a family like ours."

What made it more difficult for Mrs. Zoine was that she had recently bought twin Bob a new 1948 Dodge for $2,200. It was money that Bob had earned on his job with Kelly's and which he had been giving his mother.

"The idea was that Mom was to use it to help out around the house," Bob said. "But she saved every penny of it—and added some of the family's own money to it—when we went to buy the car."

There's a story that Bob tells about the car.

It was in the middle of summer of 1948, when Bob had a three-week vacation. He decided to spend it in the Catskills. He stored the car in a neighborhood garage in Brooklyn, and went upstairs with friends.

"When I garaged the car," Bob related, "it had 1,500 miles on the dial. When I came back and went for the car, the garage man looked at me as though I were some kind of a nut.

" 'Didn't you take the car out the day after you left it here?' the man asked me.

"Right away I guessed what had happened. Vinnie and I were twins. Although we didn't look exactly alike, there was enough of a resemblance to warrant someone making a mistake in identity. I knew Vinnie must have 'borrowed' the car.

"The bum had run it up to 2,900 miles—and burned out the motor," Bob recalled ruefully. "That was about the only time I ever really got mad at Vinnie. I could have killed him."

Vinnie just laughed.

"So what harm was there to it if I drove the car a little bit," Vinnie jested. "After all, you weren't using it."

"But the motor," howled Bob, "you've burned it out!"

Vinnie just shrugged.

"The trouble is they don't make the cars the way they used to," he kidded.

Bob was fit to be tied.

"Mom finally calmed me down and told me to sell the car," Bob said. "The best part of it was that Mom allowed me to keep all the money. I got $1,800 for the car."

Mama Julie should have been angered with Vinnie, too. But she wasn't. She couldn't get mad at her children. Mama was very worried now about Vinnie's future. The prospect of sending her son to actor's school gnawed at her until finally—

"I had a woman neighbor drive me to the city, to the Academy of Dramatic Arts. I decided I was going to find out myself what chance Vinnie had as an actor.

"I asked for the dean, who turned out to be the nicest man you'd ever want to meet. He was distinguished and grey-haired, and he greeted me with the greatest courtesy when I told him why I was there.

" 'Please tell me the truth,' I said to him, 'has my son got a chance? As Vinnie's mother, I am ready to make sacrifices and to raise the money for his tuition. We're not a family of great means. We're poor people. But if there's a chance Vinnie can make it, I am willing to do it. Please don't spare me—I must know the truth.' "

The dean took Mrs. Zoine's hand, pressed it gently.

"Your son," the dean began, "is good enough. In this school we only pick the best. Many apply but few are accepted. Vincent is qualified and he has an excellent chance to hit the top. He has many good qualities. His only drawback is a certain amount of shyness. But I'm sure he'll overcome that when he comes out of his shell and gains self-assurance. It will take a great deal of time—and perhaps you're not in a position to sacrifice that much."

Mrs. Zoine felt a lump in her throat.

"How much will it cost, sir?" she asked.

"Eight hundred dollars . . ."

Mrs. Zoine thanked the man profusely and went home.

That night, when Papa Zoine returned from work—he was still at it in construction—Mama

Julie discussed the Academy of Dramatic Arts with her husband.

"I'll even get a job to help raise the money," she told Vinnie's father. "This is the thing he wants. We have to do it for him."

Papa Zoine was not one to hold back a son of his who wanted to make a success of himself. He yielded to Mama Julie's proposition.

The next day, Mrs. Zoine went to the bank and withdrew the money.

"Here," she told Vinnie when she returned home. "This is the tuition. Now go and become an actor."

Vinnie threw his arms around his mother and held her in a bearlike hug. When Mama Julie looked up at Vinnie, she saw tiny shimmering reflections in his eyes. They were tears—matching the tears that were in her eyes that moment.

The next day, Mrs. Zoine went to the Board of Education headquarters at 210 Livingston Street in downtown Brooklyn.

"I read that you are hiring cafeteria employees," Mrs. Zoine told a woman in the personnel division. "I want a job . . ."

Mrs. Zoine filled out an application. A few weeks later, she reported for work behind the cafeteria counter at the Eli Whitney Vocational High

School in Brooklyn. Julie Zoine had found the job that would help pay for her son's tuition, which she hoped would be his ticket to Hollywood and movie stardom.

Little did she dream then that Vinnie would someday be the celebrated Dr. Ben Casey of television fame. In those days, TV was still in embryo. The Broadway stage and Hollywood were the primary goals of all the dreamy-eyed actors and actresses who were trying to crack the big-time.

With tuition in hand, Vinnie promptly enrolled in the American Academy of Dramatic Arts and became one of the slaves to the acting profession. But unlike the slaves before Lincoln and the Civil War, these denizens of the drama were dedicated and determined to work as hard is humanly possible for the great future the theatrical world held.

Few succeeded, of course. But the Fates had bestowed their blessings upon many of the students in Vinnie's class. For among his classmates, in looking back now through the pages of history, we can recognize the names in an instant—Grace Kelly, Anne Bancroft, John Cassavetes. And Vinnie Zoine!

Indeed, he was in fast company.

Vinnie attended classes in a T-shirt, for it was stylish to dress that way.

"I was not the original T-shirt actor," muses Vince Edwards today. "I guess Brando beat me out in that department. But I had it over Brando and all the others in one respect—I wore the dirtiest T-shirt of all the dirty T-shirt actors."

In truth, Vinnie couldn't afford to wear anything but a dirty T-shirt, for he was now beginning the long, struggling climb which would one day lead to his current preeminence in the entertainment world's heavens.

It was to be a dreary, dreadful, disappointing climb that would rock Vinnie with despair and frustration for eleven long and trying years.

Life is seldom easy for a young actor. Vinnie tried with all his might. He prayed that he would succeed.

Some of the people who were with Vinnie in school back in those days remember him vividly. Harry Mastrogeorge, now a dramatic coach, was in the same class with Vinnie then.

"There was nothing special about Vince back in school as I recall," Mastrogeorge says today. "I remember he turned up for most of his classes and seemed keen to get on. He was a good mixer, and was always popular at our parties."

Another comment comes from Marie Myers, a secretary at the academy, whose recollection of Vince Edwards is keener in one special area.

"The thing I remember best about him is that all the girls thought he was a *wow!* The girls simply were mad about him."

Vinnie started school in early 1949. He continued his dramatic courses right into 1950. Then one day in early May, Vinnie came home, as he'd been doing every day since he had started school. He lived with his family.

"What's wrong, son?" asked Mrs. Zoine, who by now had become accustomed to Vinnie's dour looks. "Did you find a wallet with a lot of money in it?"

Vinnie had a broad grin.

"You might say that," he practically trilled. "I've got a job! I'm going to star in a movie!"

Mrs. Zoine stepped back against the wall for support.

"Say that again, son."

The look of incredulity on Mama Julie's face was something to see.

"That's right, Mom. They're going to let me play in a picture called *Mr. Universe*. And guess what my role's going to be?"

Mrs. Zoine shook her head. She was too stunned to talk.

"You are looking," Vinnie continued with a giggle, raising his arms and tightening his fists so the muscles bulged like iron balls, "at Mr. Universe!"

Silence. Long silence. Mrs. Zoine went on staring unbelievingly at Vince.

"Me, Mom," Vinnie ranted on, "I'm in the title role—Mr. Universe."

Then, as Mrs. Zoine regained her composure, she liked for details how it happened.

"They saw me down on Broadway. Some producer. He told me I could work in the film. Be the star. But there's one catch . . ."

"What's that?" asked Mama Julie, now fully in command of her senses.

"I've got to dye my hair blond!"

Mrs. Zoine burst into paroxysm of laughter. Then came the tears, tears of happiness. She was happy for Vinnie, who had at last found his niche. Or had he?

Vinnie thought so. He was twenty-one and he had signed a contract for his first movie!

The producer was Hal Wallis. Wallis had visited the Academy to look over the crop of actors and actresses. He spotted Vinnie Zoine. Wallis liked the build. He inquired. He was told that Vinnie was a champion swimmer, a dedicated weight lifter, and a nut about organic foods.

"That kind of a guy can fill the bill as a Mr. Universe," Wallis concluded. "But can he act?" Inquiries at the school produced a favorable report on Vinnie, and he was signed.

A few nights later, Vinnie came home with the script.

"This is it," he told his twin, Bob. "Read it—see how you like it."

"When he gave me the script," Bob recalls today, "I thought it was good for laughs. I never took Vinnie's acting efforts seriously in those days. I thought it was some kind of a fantasy with him. To me it was Vinnie's way of trying to get out of working. Mama was the only one who had any faith in him."

Bob glanced through the script.

"Right away I saw the story plot—it was about a typical American boy, a regular Joe Palooka type. I wasn't impressed."

Turning to Vinnie, Bob said, "Wait'll the guys on the block see you in this—with blond hair. They'll run you out of town."

Nevertheless, Bob wished Vince well.

"Oh, by the way," Vince told his brother. "I'm changing my name—for the movies, of course."

"What moniker are you going to use—Percy Musclebound?" Bob asked jibingly.

"Nope," Vince replied. "I'm simply going to drop Zoine and use my first two names—Vincent Edwards. The only change really is the 's' on Edward. How do you like that? How does it sound—Vincent Edwards?"

"Too American," cracked Bob. "How the hell are the *paisans* going to recognize one of their own?"

Thus Vincent Edwards was born.

He was born for the new role that destiny had carved for him in the celluloid world of make-believe.

Shooting on *Mr. Universe* was ordered for June l. Vince reported with the rest of the cast, to the movie facilities at Sunnyside Gardens in Long Island City.

The cast was fairly impressive. There was Jack Carson, who was to play Jeff Claxton; Janice Paige, who was Lorraine; Bert Lahr, as Joe Pulaski, and Robert Alda, in the part of Fingers Maroni. In addition, there was former middleweight boxing champion Slapsie Maxie Rosenbloom, Joyce Matthews, singer Donald Novis, and television commentator Dennis James, all playing themselves.

Vince was given third billing, after Carson and Miss Paige. It was a tall niche for a beginner.

The story line developed by Searle Kramer, who wrote the screenplay, was aimed at panning the

83

suddenly popular wrestling profession which literally had taken over the television channels lock, stock, and barrel. Everyone was watching the beef-trust boys on the magic lantern of TV in those days. Hollywood was now beginning to feel the pinch of television and more and more movies were produced to kid video.

After shooting began, Vince came home one night and invited Bob to come out and watch him on the set.

"I had more important things to do than watch Vinnie hamming it up," Bob said. "I had recently been engaged and was busy planning out the wedding. But when he asked me to come out, I couldn't refuse. I had to see how this brother of mine was managing to keep from working at an honest living."

Actually, Vinnie was already better off than Bob. Vinnie was getting $150 a week under the terms of the contract.

"It was just like Hollywood," Bob recalls his visit to the Sunnyside sound stage. "There were the grips and electricians and scenery shifters all falling over themselves in their haste to get the set ready for the actors. It was confusion at its height—just what I expected, just like you see it in the movies.

"Then I got a glimpse of the actors. I recognized Jack Carson and Janice Paige and some of the others. I looked around for my brother. Finally I saw him, trailed by a makeup man who was slapping powder on his body.

"I laughed inside. I was wondering what the guys in the neighborhood would say if they could see Vinnie now. But I will say this about him—he really looked impressive with his massive build. I guess I was proud of him, deep down.

"But I won't change my opinion of what I saw then. I say to this day that he was a ham."

Bob's view was shared later, when the film was completed, by a number of movie reviewers. Jim O'Connor, the drama editor of the *New York Journal-American*, was one of the kinder critics who attended the premiere at the Palace Theater on Broadway on March 22, 1951.

"*Mr. Universe* is played strictly for laughs," wrote

O'Connor. "Sometimes you laugh with the picture. Sometimes you laugh at the picture. But most of the times you laugh at either one or the other."

O'Connor found the plot reasonable. It concerned a contest to choose America's best-built male. Vince Edwards won it and was crowned "Mr. Universe." Then, through the machinations and scheming of Carson, a pitchman, Edwards is converted into a wrestler made prey to the promotional genius of that master of doubletalk, Lahr.

In quick time, Edwards becomes a wrestling phenomenon. As he rises to invincibility on the nation's mats, the sport begins to suffer, Lahr and Carson decide Vince has to be tamed. They slow him down, then sell his contract to Robert Alda, a gangster. Then they proceed to bet against Mr. Universe, but in the end pull a switch and put their money on him.

"If all this sounds confusing to you," wrote O'Connor, "it's because it was confusing to me. But funny."

O'Connor blamed some of the film's failings on the low budget on which it was made, but he couldn't forgive some of the lines.

"Some of the gags," he commented, "are almost as old, as some of the wrestlers."

What did critic O'Connor think of Vince Edwards?

"As Mr. Universe," the drama editor wrote, "Vincent Edwards turns out to be a great big, good-looking kid, but no actor yet."

Vince read this review and the others, which were as critical and perhaps more unkind than O'Connor's.

Was Vince discouraged?

"Frankly, I was," the Vince Edwards of today says. "I never liked the plot in the first place. But I took it because it spelled opportunity. After I saw the picture, I was convinced I had done the wrong thing. It was a lousy way to make a debut in the movies—as a big, dumb, blond kid. That kind of a character gets you labeled."

After *Mr. Universe*, Vince Edwards went the way of all actors without friends or connections in the right places—he joined the ranks of the jobless and fell in with the queues of idle actors at the unemployment insurance window.

For a brief time, Vince found work in the Broadway musical, *High Button Shoes*. He was a chorus boy.

He wasn't happy. He wondered about his future. He wondered if anyone would ever offer him a part in movie again. It was discouraging, disillusioning.

Vince thought the whole world had forgotten him.

But fortunately, it would seem, one person remembered him. That was Hal Wallis, who hadn't quite given up Vince.

"I want you to come out to Hollywood," Wallis told him one day when Vince was sulking over his career's misfortunes. "I've got big things planned for you."

Suddenly, Vince was on Cloud Nine.

He floated home on that cloud and lifted his mother off her feet.

"Mom, Mom," he shouted in triumph, "guess what's happened—I'm going to Hollywood!"

Vince told his family about Wallis' offer.

They were all thrilled. That night there was a celebration. A big dinner and toasts of rich red vino to Vinnie, who was on his way to the tinseled city of filmdom to become a great star.

Little did they know or, for that matter, did Vince know what Hal Wallis had in mind. If Vince had known he would not have allowed himself to leave New York.

With hopes as high as they'd ever been in his life, Vincent Edwards headed for Hollywood.

5
HOLLYWOOD

ALL HIS LIFE, in Brooklyn, Vince Edwards stood on his rights as a human being and fought the battles facing him with raw courage and unbending nerve. He never let anyone step on him. He never allowed anyone to *use* him.

In Hollywood, suddenly, Vince was confronted with the dreadful realization that he was sucked into one of the movie industry's oldest stratagems—the so-called dead-ringer gambit.

Wallis had brought Vince out to the film city because he had the same general appearance as one of Paramount's biggest stars, Burt Lancaster.

Edwards' role became crystal clear to him some months after he got a call one day to report to the studio.

Vince showed up bright and early, eagerness swelling inside him for work.

"Get ready," he was told, "we're going to put you into *Come Back, Little Sheba*."

Vince was overwhelmed. Everything he had read in the columns, everything he had heard down at Schwab's Drugs Store on Sunset Strip; the gathering place of the Hollywood hopefuls, had indicated that the mighty Burt Lancaster had been designated for the role in this film.

But Lancaster had balked at doing *Come Back, Little Sheba*. The studio was forced to seek a replacement and Vince Edwards was that replacement.

Little did Vince know then that the old dead-ringer gambit was being played by the studio—to get Lancaster to sign up.

The strategy works this way: After the star balks, the producer goes to him and says, "Okay, Burt, you don't have to play in the picture. I've got a kid named Vincent Edwards who's got a lot on the ball. He's almost a dead-ringer for you. We'll let him take your part, and just watch him go. This picture will make him. He'll be bigger than you ever were."

As it is customary to play this game, the sucker—Edwards in this case—is kept in the dark about his actual role in the film. Nobody tells him that he's the pawn.

Vince reported obediently to Wallis' office every day for two whole months, wondering, waiting, wringing his hands with impatience to get started. Every day someone would tell him, "We're still working out the details—come back tomorrow." And on the morrow Vince would be back.

After two months passed, Vince came in one day to learn the truth.

"Lancaster just changed his mind," he was told. "He'll do the picture. So we won't need you anymore. Sorry, but thanks for waiting around . . ."

It was Vince Edwards' first Hollywood heartbreak. There were to be many, many others before he would finally find his place in the Hall of Fame of TV-land as Dr. Ben Casey.

Vince was swept out into the street, so to speak, and there he joined the army of young hopefuls who roam Hollywood like wolfpacks, looking for employment before the cameras, hanging around drive-in restaurants and drugstores like Schwab's, waiting for a call, taking whatever odd jobs that acting can offer until the big break comes along.

Looking back on those difficult times today, Vince says, "I was too young and naive to be discouraged. Besides, I was dedicated. I wanted to make something of myself. Nothing else mattered."

Vince shudders when he recalls his experience with *Come Back, Little Sheba*. But that wasn't his only run-in with the studio moguls who almost signed him for a big part.

In an interview with Marcia Borie in *Modern Screen Magazine*, Vince recalled how he almost got the lead role in another film classic, *On the Waterfront*.

"I was supposed to star in that," Vince said. "I was very friendly with the writer, Budd Shulberg. I was on the ground floor with him and Elia Kazan, who was to direct it. I was always around them. I was the guy who was supposed to do the lead. And I delivered the first copy of the script to Jerry Wald, at four o'clock in the morning. You know what happened? It's all part of history now. They decided they needed a name: Marlon Brando."

All his life in Brooklyn, Vince Edwards stood on his rights as a human being and fought the battles that faced him with raw courage and unbending nerve. He never let anyone step on him. He never allowed anyone to use him.

But he was in Hollywood now. Human dignity and human rights don't mean much to the studio titans whose only aim in life is to produce pictures and make money. They care not a hoot about anyone's feelings nor does it grieve them when they break someone's heart. The tragic part of it all is that the victims—the guys like Vincent Edwards who are trampled on—have no recourse. They have to stay and take it. Of course, they have one alternative. That's to get out of Hollywood.

But Vince Edwards didn't want to get out. He was never a quitter. He was going to stay and fight—and do his damndest to win.

As a member now of Hollywood's well-known "Legion of Almosts," Vince could gather at Schwaberino's an address his fellow struggling actors like Caesar addressing his fellow Romans.

"Friends and fellow sufferers," he would say. "Lend me your sympathy. I almost got Burt Lancaster's part in *Come Back, Little Sheba*. And they almost gave me Marlon Brando's part in *On the Waterfront*. Yeah, I was almost a star."

That was the extent of any distinction he could lay claim to—unless he wanted to take credit for the fact that he had once co-starred in *Mr. Universe*. But that was a picture Vince Edwards would not ever mention. He preferred to let it be forgotten.

Hollywood can be a bleak, unfriendly place to the unemployed actor. Hollywood was bleak and unfriendly to Vince Edwards. However, it was not a complete disaster. At least Vince managed to work now and then.

It wasn't much, but it helped to keep him from starving. The jobs were a conglomeration of insignificant parts in television. He appeared in one production of *General Electric Theater* and on another of *Alfred Hitchcock Presents*. He also did bit parts for theatrical stock companies and once, belatedly, was given the lead in a road company production of *Come Back, Little Sheba*. It wasn't the same as playing the movie version, which Burt Lancaster did, but it was work. It kept the wolf from the door.

Other small parts came along. Most of them were roles of crooks and killers. And most of the times Vince Edwards was shot and killed to the delight of audiences.

He was three thousand miles from Brooklyn and the city of his birth was happily forgetting the dread days of machine-gun fire and gangland rides when Murder, Inc. dominated the scene as the ruling syndicate of the underworld. But the racketing bark of tommy-gun bullets were constantly exploding around Vince Edwards in Hollywood. It was better getting shot with film city blanks than by the lethal guns of the old Brooklyn mob.

But what kind of a future is there for an actor who keeps getting shot up in film after film?

Vince wondered about it more and more.

Back home, his mother and father thought about it, too. Was this what they had spent their hard-earned money for? To send their son to school to learn dramatics—only to end up acting in roles that needed no dramatic training? Murder, Inc.'s mobsters used to drop dead like flies and they never had any formal training for it. They died for real. How much training does a guy need to drop dead?

These were awkward and embarrassing times for Vince. He couldn't justify his course in Hollywood to his mother and father. There was nothing he could say to vindicate his expensive schooling for a *nothing* job in Hollywood.

Vince was desperate and disgusted.

He had built up his hopes on Hollywood and a film career. He had switched his plans and sought new goals when he had lost faith in the old ones.

Could he change his plans and goals again? What was left?

No, Vince decided he'd stick to the plot no matter how difficult to follow. He'd give Hollywood a chance. Deep down inside he felt there was a special niche in the cinematic heavens for him. It was just a matter of finding his way there, he told himself.

As 1952 rolled around, Vince was scrounging around for anything that would pay his rent and buy his food. In desperation, he took a job as a singer in a Hollywood nightclub. It was a small club and the pay was commensurate to the size of the establishment. But it helped Vince negotiate the whirling rapids which had been threatening to hurl him upon the rocks of starvation.

Then a break came. Hal Wallis and Allied Artists approached Vince with an offer to appear in an adventure film entitled *Hiawatha*, based on the famous poem. Vince was offered the lead. He grabbed it. It was a break but it didn't mean anything in the end. The picture was shot on a low budget and never met any serious acclaim to speak of. Nevertheless, it gave Vince encouragement and hope. At least he had two films under his belt now. Maybe others would come along.

Meanwhile, during his long stretches of idleness, the hopeful thespian from the sidewalks of Brooklyn took to his first love—swimming. Whenever he found the time—and he had plenty of time—Vince headed out for the gleaming white sands of Malibu where he would ply through the surf to his heart's content, often wondering as he did if he shouldn't have stayed home in Brooklyn and pursued his original ambition to be a great swimmer. His appendix, which had forced him out of competition in the Olympics, had given him no more trouble.

"I wondered if I trained again whether I might not make the Olympic team," Vince said. "I was still only twenty-two and stronger than ever."

But Malibu is no place for an Olympic candidate to train. It's better suited for a guy to show off his muscles—as Vince did. He didn't have to try because he had the muscles to show. They didn't name the place Muscle Beach because of Vince, but his presence enhanced its reputation.

A guy with a build like Vince's is more than likely to attract girls. Vince attracted them. Not just ordinary girls but girls with charm and beauty and standing in the Hollywood film spectrum. There were, for example, Cleo Moore and Sandra Giles.

"Dames were never a problem with Vince," related an intimate who knew Vince back in those days. "He wasn't much for going out on the town or busting into parties. But he always managed to go on quiet dates with some of the town's prettiest and shapeliest starlets or stars. Sometimes the dates were set up by his agent, or the girl's, for publicity purposes. But most of the time Vince took the girls out because he simply liked the girls and the girls went for him."

I asked his twin brother if this report on Vince reflected a metamorphosis in his character or whether he had always been sweet on the fair sex.

"Vinnie," Bob replied, "was more of the ladies' man than I was and he used to date more than me. I was more on the shy-side with girls until I met Pearl (his wife whom he married in 1951). I think Vinnie dated for the first time when he was thirteen. He took the girl to the corner for a soda and then walked her home. She was a sweet kid and every bit of eleven years old.

"But, seriously, Vinnie had quite a share of the girls after he reached his middle teens. The girls seemed to go for him in a big way—even in those days."

Mama Julie Zoine was more expressive about her famous son's proclivities with girls.

"They were always chasing after Vinnie," Mama Julie told me. "They used to write him letters and postcards all the time, asking for dates. Vinnie would take them out but I don't think girls interested him that much then. He had his weight lifting and swimming to keep him occupied."

Bob listened to his mother, then turned to me, winked, and cracked, "What she doesn't know won't hurt her . . ."

In that year of 1952 in Hollywood, Vince certainly had his pick of girls and his interest in them never seemed to waver. Aside from those already mentioned, there were three others in whom Vince had taken more than a casual interest—Shelley Winters, Lizbeth Scott, and Marilyn Monroe!

His fling with Shelley Winters, who is several summers older than Vince, was perhaps the briefest but stormiest of his escapades with the women in his life. Their friendship seemed to have ended one night when Vince stormed out of a Hollywood restaurant after an argument, leaving Shelley alone midst the double orders of roast beef au jus and mashed potatoes.

A columnist who took note of this event, commented, "Just when it seems that newcomer Vince Edwards is the number one man in the life of this gal, Shelley surprises everyone by resuming with her old flame Sidney Chaplin."

Maybe Sidney had a milder temperament than Vince—and not quite as much muscle.

Some Hollywood flacks may tell you that his dates with Liz Scott were for publicity purposes.

The truth of it is Liz didn't need Vince, a relative unknown, to enhance her popularity, for she already was an established star. On the other hand, being seen with Liz might have been helpful in promoting Vince to the movie fans—if the movie fans had a chance to see them together. But Liz and Vince were not shown together in pictures in those days.

Today, in Vince's album, you can see some memorable photos of himself with Liz. You may also have seen the pictures already in some of the fan magazines. The pictures were shot by writer Nancy Streebeck, who had dropped in one Sunday afternoon in 1952 to interview Liz Scott.

Liz was on the lawn in shorts, white gloves covering her hands. She was painting the lawn furniture. With her was a hulking, handsome young man. When Liz introduced the man to Miss Streebeck, the name didn't mean a thing to her.

"He's a grocery delivery boy," Liz told Miss Streebeck in jest. "He dropped by to bring my order from the store and I kept him here to earn some extra money by painting the furniture."

Vince was in a pair of slacks, stripped to the waist. His huge hairy chest and muscular frame impressed Miss Streebeck.

"I think," Liz advised Miss Streebeck, "that you ought to take some pictures and keep them on file.

Someday Vince is going to be a very famous delivery boy."

Miss Streebeck snapped pictures of Liz and Vince in variety of poses on the lawn working together with paint and brush on the furniture.

Liz had more faith in Vince than the magazine editors of those days. They turned down the pictures. But Miss Streebeck kept the negatives on file. Recently, after the Ben Casey explosion, Miss Streebeck dug down deep for those negatives and found plenty of magazine editors willing to take them at almost any price she cared to quote.

Vince continued to see Liz and Cleo and Sandra.

And Marilyn Monroe, too.

When I wrote Marilyn Monroe's biography, I said she was introduced to Joe DiMaggio by Hollywood business agent David March. That was how it happened in mid-March of 1952. But my research on Vince Edwards reveals the role big Vince had in making it all possible.

The year was 1950. Marilyn had yet to realize the fruition of her dreams in her early desperate years of struggle for stardom. She was part of the great legion of unemployed hopefuls tramping the pavements in an endless, turbulent promenade from studio to studio in pursuit of the one big break. Vince was in the same shoes.

Fate, perhaps, had brought them together, bivouacked in the same office at Twentieth Century-Fox. They sat opposite each other in the casting director's crowded ante-room, patiently sweating out a call from the inner sanctum. Anxiety, tension, nervousness charged the atmosphere.

From his tight little chair, the hulking, handsome actor regarded the gorgeous blonde across from him with intense masculine curiosity. He sensed somehow the volcano simmering beneath the spectacular beauty his eyes took in.

He stared. Their eyes met. Suddenly he detected a smidgeon of a smile edging her lips. Fed by the spark of this fleeting recognition, Vince returned a pleasant, sympathetic smile and mimicked a mute "hello" with his lips. She returned the greeting the same way. They turned from each other and let their glances stray aimlessly around the room.

A door opened finally and a girl came out. "That's all for today," she said with cast-iron stillness reflecting the coldness and indifference Hollywood holds for the lowly and downtrodden. Their hopes dashed again, the expectant actors and actresses filed slowly out of the room to await another day.

"It's rough, isn't it?" Vince said as Marilyn edged up to him in the crowded corridor to the street.

Marilyn looked at Vince. A smile again brightened her sad face. She had been fighting all her life. The disappointments and frustrations were like mountains penning her in a deep valley. Defeat upon defeat had failed to dull her incentive, but there were times when the edge would wear away. Someone like Vince now seemed to sharpen Marilyn's spirits.

"It's always the same story, isn't it?" Marilyn said demurely. "We all wait for that one chance."

"It'll come," Vince said confidently. "But it takes time."

Little did Vince know how prophetic his statement was. Speaking for himself, that is. For, as we all know, it was soon after this that Marilyn found her place in Hollywood and climbed those majestic peaks from which she, reigned as prime goddess in Hollywood's pagan pantheon.

For Vince it would take longer; years of agonizing waiting. Eleven years, actually.

"I have an appointment over at Paramount," Vince offered casually as he walked into the bright midday sunshine with Marilyn. "Want to come along?"

102

Vince was due at Hal Wallis' office. He was still on their dead-ringer gambit. He followed orders, reporting every day to receive word when he would be signed to play in *Come Back, Little Sheba*. Six weeks or more passed, now and Vince decided he'd better try his luck at some of the other studios, just in case the promised deal at Paramount fell through. That's how he happened to be at Fox that morning.

"Do you really think you'll get the part?" Marilyn asked Vince after he gave her a rundown on his activities.

"You live in hope in this town," Vince murmured. "It's gotten so you have to keep up the faith. Lose it—lose yourself."

The answer at Paramount was routine to Vince by now. "Come back tomorrow."

There was nothing there for Marilyn either.

They became friends, Marilyn and Vince, at times bumping into each other at various casting offices. Other times they met at modest Hollywood parties or the usual places where struggling actors and actresses meet, like Schwab's.

Eventually, Vince asked Marilyn to go out. They dated infrequently, but they dated. It wasn't romance, just friendship, according to those who are close to Vince. For in those days Vince couldn't afford to be romantic or to get involved with dames in love.

Yet their friendship blossomed into a strong ca-maraderie that ensued through the years which saw Marilyn zoom to stardom, while Vince remained a struggling actor clawing his way tenaciously to what ultimately would be television stardom as the mighty Dr. Ben Casey.

During those years, Marilyn often confided in Vince Edwards. And he confided in her. They discussed their mutual problems and, though they were poles apart in their careers, they found very often that their problems were not dissimilar.

There was this big difference, however, as the year 1962 ironically would prove. Vince had the wherewithal to conquer his problems. Tragically, Marilyn could not solve hers.

But in 1952 they were a long time away from Vince's spectacular breakthrough. His name was not yet a household word in millions of homes across the land. They were a long time away from the spectre of tragic death that would claim Marilyn at the peak of her greatness.

In mid-March of 1952 they were more than a decade away from that point in time.

But Fortune had begun to smile down on Mar-ilyn by then. She made *Asphalt Jungle* and emerged as the film capital's next potential cheesecake queen, the girl who'd replace Lana Turner and Betty Grable, the then still-reigning queens. Quickly she was pushed into *All About Eve, As Young as You Feel, Let's Make it Legal, Clash by Night* and *Don't Bother to Knock*. She was given the Big Buildup which meant literally posing for thousands of studio publicity shots. In no time Marilyn was appearing on the covers of national magazines and in newspapers in every city and hamlet in the country.

Among the kaleidoscope of poses was one of Marilyn taken in Pasadena during the 1951 spring baseball training season. Marilyn posed in shorts at bat with Chicago White Sox fielder Gus Zernial, who was showing her how to take her stance at the plate.

The picture caught the eye of Joe DiMaggio, the New York Yankees' great outfielder who had just retired from the sport at the age of thirty-seven. He remembered the girl and her name a year later when he came to Los Angeles and met his friend David March, the Hollywood business agent.

March and Joe were talking. March happened to mention that Marilyn Monroe was a personal friend.

"I'd like to meet her," Joe told March. l

"I think I can fix up a date for you," March offered.

The story I had gotten originally for Marilyn's biography was that March phoned Marilyn and arranged for her to come down to the Villa Nova and have dinner with the Yankee Clipper. But I have since discovered it was Vince Edwards who actually made the date with Marilyn.

Vince had always been a baseball fan and DiMaggio was one of his favorites. When he was approached to make contact with Marilyn in Joe's behalf, he was glad to oblige. Vince and Joe had two things in common—a passion for baseball and their Italian ancestry. And when they met that evening at the Villa Nova with March, they found plenty to talk about in the two hours they sat at the table waiting for Marilyn.

Marilyn was late as always—but she finally arrived.

After dinner and drinks and a long evening of conversation, Marilyn leaned over and whispered to Vince, "He wants me to take him to his hotel in my car. I don't mind. I think he's nice."

Vince winked approvingly.

"Go ahead," he said. "He's a swell guy."

And that's how Marilyn Monroe met Joe DiMaggio, who would in time become her husband, then her ex-husband but, still, as time would prove, the only man who really loved Marilyn heart and soul.

This is a brief interlude in Vince Edwards' life but, as we contemplate his past, a highly significant one.

6
BEHIND THE SCENES

THE VAGUEST PART of Vincent Edwards' life as an actor is the period from 1952 through 1959. It's as though he lived those seven years in a vacuum or time capsule. Of all the millions of words written about him in newspapers, magazines, and studio releases, virtually no details ever mention that time in his life as an actor when Vince was bucking for the big break in movies. You rarely find even a mention or listing of the nearly score of movies in which he portrayed a variety of killers, psychopaths, and other villainous characters.

There were more of those, actually, than there were Dr. Ben Casey shows in the first half of the 1961-'62 season which catapulted Vince to his mystical medical throne on Mount Olympus. Yet none of those Hollywood films gave Vince the lift-off he needed to put him into orbit around the cinematic world. The thrust just wasn't there.

But Vince would not be discouraged.

"I don't talk much about those days," Vince admits. "I. guess I was too young and naive and discouragement for me was hard to come by. Moreover, I was dedicated. I wanted to make something of myself and I wouldn't let anything stop my drive."

Ask Vince about his film work in those years and he tells you: "I had a name, but it wasn't the right one. Other guys, it always seemed, had bigger names. That was what the studios wanted—a big name. I couldn't make it big because the parts I had didn't lend themselves to stardom. They were like character builders. They gave me experience and know-how and a living wage. But nothing else, except perhaps hope.

"I wouldn't give up. I felt I had to stick at it. Every day someone I knew who'd been in the same fix as myself made it big. I kept saying that my break will come, I've got to hold on. I watched a lot of guys make it—Jim Garner, Steve McQueen, Chuck Connors, John Cassavetes—and I told myself, 'Stick with it. Your chance will come.' But it took twelve years. That's a long time."

During his undistinguished era in movies as a mobster and murderer, Vince Edwards must have killed as many people as he's saved as the dedicated but ill-tempered Dr. Casey on video.

His first vehicles into filmland mayhem were either insignificant in themselves as pictures or insignificant because of the amount of screen exposure afforded Vince. Sometimes he had barely a minute's time on the screen, although his part was fairly considerable to begin with. He was a victim of the cutting room where the frames of the film showing him inevitably ended up.

As Vince struggled to get recognition—to get *somewhere*—he gallivanted about town as a "hot-shot" and a "ladies' man."

He continued to see Lizbeth Scott who, although beautiful, was older than Vince. She evidently was his number one girl until, as the Hollywood rumor mill puts it, Liz told Vince she was in love with someone else.

He then turned his attentions to Jackie Loughery, a Brooklynite like Vince. She had come west to compete in the Miss Universe contest in 1952. Jackie, who was Miss New York State, won the title of Miss United States but was beaten in the finals.

Jackie had met Guy Mitchell and married him, but less than a year later it was all over. In getting her divorce Jackie testified that Guy "thought more of his horse than of me." After the divorce, which brought her $1,500-a month alimony, Jackie started seeing Vince. They did the town together and made the Tablehoppers one of their favorite rendezvous.

According to the gossip around Hollywood and Vine, Vince is supposed to have fallen in love with Jackie—and even bought a ring for her. Jackie had told interviewers, "I'm looking for a guy who wants a wife and twelve kids." Everyone thought Vince would be the guy. But, as the yarn goes, Jackie wouldn't wear the ring.

And that was the end of the "romance." Jackie later married Jack Webb.

From Jackie, Vince turned to Rosemary Webster, a dancer. A column on the Coast printed an item that Vince and Rosemary were going to get married, and even published the date—September 21, 1953. Moreover, the writer went so far as to say the honeymoon was all set for Hawaii.

That never happened, for Vince went right on as a roaming bachelor playing the whole, delectable field of starlets and stars which Hollywood was noted for. And he seemed to play it strictly for fun.

His only serious side was his acting. He was still looking for the big break.

It wasn't until 1954 that Vince got his first chance to dig his teeth into a part in a Metro Goldwyn Mayer film, *Rogue Cop*.

This was an important production for it brought together a great cast, led off by Robert Taylor, Janet Leigh, George Raft, Steve Forrest, and Anne Francis. Vince Edwards, playing Langley, a hoodlum, was six places down from Miss Francis on the cast sheet. Nevertheless, it was a part with substance for Vince.

Bosley Crowther, who reviewed the picture for the *New York Times* after its opening in the New York Paramount, said, "This is not a new thesis. They've been making movies on it for years, and

Rogue Cop is not so exceptional in its construction or performance that it is likely to cause a surprise. But it is a well-done melodrama, produced and directed in a hard, crisp style, and it is very well acted by Robert Taylor in the somewhat disagreeable title role."

Disagreeable title role!

No one agree more with that definition than Vince Edwards' mother. She could have killed Taylor for what he did to her son, but let's begin from the beginning.

The picture's plot involves a crooked cop in gangster killings, with violence as the keynote. Taylor plays police sergeant Christopher Kelvaney, a hard-boiled cop in the way of the crime syndicate headed by Dan Beaumonte, played by George Raft, naturally.

When one of the latter's homicidal henchmen is arrested by Kelvaney's younger brother, Eddie (Steve Forrest), an honest patrolman, the syndicate orders Taylor to bribe his brother into dropping the case. The rookie refuses to sell out and despite all the sergeant's efforts to save his brother, the young patrolman is killed.

Who killed him?

Vince Edwards, of course.

The murder prompts Sergeant Kelvaney to turn against his erstwhile bosses. He sets out to avenge his brother's death.

In the climactic scene, Taylor wallops Edwards from pillar to post and leaves him a bleeding pulp.

"Mom, Mom," Vince said excitedly over the long-distance phone after the film was released, "Go and see *Rogue Cop*. You'll see your son in a great role!"

It was not unusual for Vince to call his mother in Brooklyn.

"In all the years Vinnie was out in Hollywood," Mama Julie Zoine told me, "he never once failed to call me each week. He is a wonderful boy."

When Vince told his mother to see *Rogue Cop*, she went and saw it with spirits higher than the Williamsburgh Savings Bank Building, Brooklyn's tallest structure. But when she had left the theater, her mood was deeper than the Brooklyn-Battery Tunnel under the East River.

Mrs. Zoine didn't wait for the following week to hear from her son. She called him that very night.

"Vinnie," she wept in the receiver, "don't you ever tell me to go and see another movie like that again."

"Why, Mom?" Vince asked in bewilderment.

"I'm all broken up. My chest is aching. My heart is torn in little pieces . . ."

"Why, why, Mom?" Vince persisted.

"I know you killed Robert Taylor's brother in the picture, but I thought it was terrible the way he treated you . . ."

"How's that, Ma?"

"Every punch he gave you—I felt it on my own body."

"But, Ma, it's only make-believe. It's only acting."

"I don't care. Make-believe or not, I can't stand to see you beaten up. I used to like Robert Taylor. He was my favorite actor until tonight. Now I hate him!"

Vince laughed delightedly.

Delightedly because if the impression left on his mother could have half that effect on movie fans, Vince Edwards would win the following he needed to put him in starring roles.

The fans didn't react. Vince remained mired in the deadly quicksand of mediocrity, plodding along in plots that left the fans cold or indifferent—and his mother heartsick.

"He was either killing or being killed," she said. "I finally called him one day and said to Vinnie,

'Why don't they give you a picture where you can make love or something?'

" 'Just wait Mom,' he replied 'there'll be one someday.' "

Zoine also told me that she actually stopped seeing her son's gangster films.

"I couldn't take it," she related mournfully. "It was too much for his mother."

Even though Mama Julie couldn't stand the horrors of murder and mayhem on screen, Vince went on with those roles. Sometimes he couldn't stand to see his own image being mowed down by gangster bullets—but it was the only way he could work and stay in Hollywood.

He was in a rut.

But he got paid and he was in demand, and Vince knew he had a chance to get somewhere. Someday.

It didn't come for Vince in his next screen role in *The Night Holds Terror*. No one could expect him to emerge as a star from this film, which was crippled by a bad plot.

It was the old familiar theme—three murderous hoodlums who invade the home of a nice young couple, create expected panic, and lead into the conventional hair-breadth hostage kidnaping at the end.

The picture had two quick strikes against it, for at the time most of its cast, except John Cassavetes, were virtual unknowns. Its stars were Jack "Maverick" Kelly and Hildy Parks. Cassavetes, who was known better then for his fine acting roles on television, was third in the billing. Vince Edwards was fourth—not bad.

The *New York Times* movie critic who saw *The Night Holds Terror* at a Loew's neighborhood theaters' showcase premiere, gave the film a favorable review despite the fact that it was, as he called it, "a bare-handed, low-budget entry."

Commenting about individual performances, the reviewer noted that Cassavetes did "quite well" and Miss Parks was "really outstanding." But in the general critique, the man from the *Times* found that Kelly and Miss Parks, and their tormentors "are all much too young, and only one of the entire five, burly Vince Edwards, looks capable of swatting a fly."

That was all the notice Vince rated. And where did it leave him? No further than when he played *Mr. Universe*, which had created that image. He was still "Mr. Muscles" to Hollywood and to the small segment of film fans who took heed of Vince Edwards.

There were long weeks and months between jobs. He had to make nickels and even pennies stretch.

"I went through the Rice Krispies bit for so long," Vince says, "that I thought I'd turn into a bowl of cereal myself."

Meanwhile, Vince wasn't doing anything to submerge the image he had stamped on the film capital. His jaunts to Malibu's Muscle Beach went right on and by 1955 he had a firmly established reputation as a "muscular nut." Helping to shape that image was Vince's occasional displays of temper at parties where he'd flatten a rival with one punch.

He also took up some spare-time hobbies which prompted many a citizen of Hollywood to speculate on the possible longevity that would accrue to Vince.

When he was a boy, Vince had an idea he wanted to be an airplane mechanic. He took up aviation in high school. At home, he was a frantic model plane enthusiast. Now in Hollywood, Vince actually turned to the sport of flying.

His friend, actor Robert Francis, helped to restore Vince's interest in flying and ultimately ushered him behind the stick in the cockpit. Vince flew solo and got to like it so well he thought about buying his own plane—someday when he could afford it.

But his interest in flying took a swift and tragic dive when Francis was killed in a crash. Vince never wanted to look at another plane after that.

For a time, Vince turned his attentions to motorcycles and became a member briefly of the black leather jacket fraternity which roared down Highway 101 in shuddering, hair-raising excursions that left citizens shaken and shorn of their sensibilities. He also raced in competition and earned a few dollars in prize money.

But his interest in cycling was short-lived. He gave it up when he realized he could not enhance his reputation—nor his lifespan—if he persisted in this pathological pursuit.

Since his appearance in *The Night Holds Terror*, Vince was working under a low-budget Columbia contract which provided a buffer between survival and starvation. The bit parts between the better parts in Grade-B movies kept his confidence buoyed and his head above water, although at times it seemed the rough currents would pull him down.

"During those years," Vince says, "I was a paraphrase of that old cliche 'always a bridesmaid, never a bride.' I'd hear one day that the studio was interested in me for a big part in a great picture. I'd say to myself, 'Oh boy, I've got it made now.' But before it would be sewed up, I'd be told, 'Sorry, Vince, they decided on a big name.'

"I had more near—misses than almost anyone."

It was that way when Columbia was casting for *Picnic*.

"Sit down, fellow," Vince was told by the casting director, "I think I've got a spot for you."

The spot, incredibly enough, was the lead in the film classic which starred Kim Novak.

Vince's hopes were high now. But he had enough good sense to leave himself an escape hatch, so that if he were turned down for a "big name," he could open a parachute and cushion his plunge. He kept telling himself, "Don't believe them, don't believe them—let it come as a surprise if it comes."

Vince sat back and waited. He had good reason to adopt this attitude. He had been stung before by sky-high promises which raised his hopes, then dashed them against the jagged crevices of a final turndown when someone else got the part.

Vince read that William Holden had been paired with Kim Novak for the leads in *Picnic*. So he wondered about Columbia's motives in telling him that he would be the star. Yet he didn't dare question the studio's intentions. He was willing to wait. And he waited for weeks.

Finally he was told. Holden signed.

Actually, Vince again had been used as a pawn, a lever to force Holden to toe the line. The star had lost interest in the picture and balked at making it. So Edwards was projected into the discussions as Holden's replacement.

But once the studio called Holden in and tossed Edwards' name at him, Bill quickly signed.

One good thing came out of his test for *Picnic*. Columbia gave Vince a $250-a-week contract!

The year 1956 brought Vince Edwards action in one film of note and several of dubious quality. The good one was *The Killing*, which starred Sterling Hayden. Vince co-starred with Coleen Gray and Jay C. Flippen. This is a story about the planning and execution of a two-million-dollar race track robbery, based on the Lionel White novel, *Clean Break*.

The film, which opened at the Mayfair in Times Square, provided eighty-three minutes of suspense and action for movie fans, and received excellent comments from critics. But although Vince enjoyed third billing in the cast of characters, the reviewers failed to take much note of him.

Rose Pelswick, writing in the *Journal-American*, simply kissed off Vince—and some of the other actors—with this brief observation: "The actors play their parts in just the right key. Assisting Hayden in a well-chosen company are Coleen Gray, Vince Edwards, Jay C. Flippen, Marie Windsor, Elisha Cook, Ted DeCorsia, and Joe Sawyer."

A. H. Weiler, who reviewed the picture for the *Times*, was a shade more generous—also more critical—with his attention to individuals.

". . . Jay C. Flippen, as an aging member of the gang, Ted DeCorsia, as a corrupt cop; Vince Edwards, as Miss Windsor's boyfriend, and Coleen Gray, as Mr. Hayden's fiancé, are interesting but not new types."

The film didn't raise Vince Edwards' stock on the Hollywood exchange. Nor did *Hit and Run* which opened, imprudently enough, in Vince's hometown theater, the Brooklyn Metropolitan.

"Cleo Moore and Hugo Haas, who have survived at least four joint movie ventures, are tempting fate anew with *Hit and Run*, a drama in which Haas is again the author, star, producer, and director."

That was Dorothy Masters' opening of her review in the *New York Daily News*. Miss Masters evidently had honed her typewriter keys to stiletto sharpness, for she snapped out words that really cut.

"They are a curious team in that the sexy Miss Moore hardly bothers to act at all, and that Haas, a recruit from the stage, has never lost a tendency to overplay. This does not, unfortunately, guarantee a happy medium."

By contrast, the hero of this biography came away smelling of roses after Miss Masters' words hit print.

"Vince Edwards lends some semblance of credulity to the affair, although he is at a disadvantage in that his characterization is unconvincingly scripted."

The year was 1957. That was the year the Zoine family lost Mary, Vince's oldest sister. She came down with walking pneumonia and died. She was the third of Mama Julie's seven children to pass away. Helen died when she was two and Carl when he was thirty-two. Mary was forty-two.

Vince came home for the funeral, then returned to Hollywood to resume the grind of trying to become a movie star.

By now, television was the new giant of the entertainment world and Vince, more and more, was keeping an eager eye focused on it. He had done a lot of work in television, but none of it exceptionally noteworthy.

He had appeared in an *Alfred Hitchcock Presents* drama, co-starred with Carol Lynley, and a *General Electric Theater* melodrama, as well as a number of other major productions in which he received limitless exposure on millions of television screens. Vince began to like the cathode tube. It provided him opportunity to be seen by vaster audiences than many of his movies. Yet he still struggled for recognition and success in Hollywood. That's what he really wanted.

The next year, 1958, saw Vince continue to perform in movies and television, but the year was notable most of all for his performance in *Murder by Contract*, a film nominated by the *Saturday Review* as "sleeper of the year." Actually, the picture did not break box-office records, but it was a commercial success.

For Vince it meant more work in more Columbia films, notably *City of Fear*, which brought him into 1959 as a veteran of nearly a decade in Hollywood—but still far from the lofty success and great wealth that he had envisioned.

He was always broke and his debts were mounting alarmingly. Vince looked around the tinseled city that had been his home for nearly ten years and took stock of himself.

"I saw what was happening," Vince related. "I had been a regular gung-ho boy. I had run through the gamut of Hollywood playboy stuff—dating starlets, showing the muscles on the beach, flying planes, motorcycling, water skiing, and all that other wild stuff.

"I realized I'd wasted some of the best years of my life. My stay in Hollywood had been unfruitful by the standards I had set for myself. I didn't know what to do."

As he struggled with himself in the mist of uncertainty and doubt that had descended around him, Vince heard a voice call. It was six thousand miles away. A voice from Hong Kong, summoning him to the Far East for a small acting role.

"Maybe this is it," Vince said to himself. "Maybe this will end my struggle once and for all. I might get lost in one of those exotic lands out there where everything isn't measured by our standards—in terms of dollars and cents and big names . . ."

It was an all-expenses-paid trip, so why not?

7
SAYONARA

'All my life I shall remember Oriental music and you in my arms; perfumed flowers in your tresses; lotus-scented breezes and swaying palms . . .

—Australian foot-soldiers' ballad

IT STILL LINGERS warmly, in exquisite detail, in Vince Edwards' memory, Japan stretched out before him in all its opiate timelessness. The scent of lotus was indeed everywhere, and so were teashops and rickshaws and all the wonders of the Orient.

And above all Michiko was there.

Michiko, a strange and wonderful girl who gave him love and brought him, almost, to the end of his career as an actor.

His trip to the Orient was, of course, purely business in the beginning. Perhaps, too, it was an escape. It was late 1958 and, with contract in hand, he'd zoomed out to Manila, then Hong Kong for what was a small part in a Grade B picture with a low-cost budget. How he made out in this film wouldn't matter to his future.

A studio executive told Vince when it was over: "You've earned a vacation. Take it easy a while. You might not get to this part of the world again for a long time. Look around. Enjoy things."

The idea appealed to the fatigued actor. He had only been out as far as Hawaii previously, and he'd always had a hankering to see Japan. Now, he decided, would be the perfect time to do it.

Vince picked Tokyo, Japan's capital, the most populous metropolis in the world, a teeming city ahum with all the vibrations of life. Vince put up at a smart hotel and began touring the town by rickshaw. One of his stops was a teashop often frequented by Americans and Europeans. He liked the food there the first time, and made a mental note to come back. On his second visit there, he met someone whose words to this day exert a powerful influence on the rising star.

It was the most improbable place in the world to meet him, but there he was, a towering mountain of a man, shoveling the food in his mouth bulldozer fashion. Vince himself had to look twice. It was he, all right. There couldn't be any question about it. Not two tables away was the great cinematic genius Orson Welles.

"I was never a backward guy," Vince recalled later. "I put the menu down, got up and walked over to him. 'Mr. Welles,' I said, 'may I introduce myself? I'm Vince Edwards . . . an actor.'

"I don't know what kind of reaction I expected from him. Maybe just a 'how do you do' and that's all. But he was genuinely pleased to meet me and nothing would do but that I sit down and join him for lunch."

Vince began by telling Welles what he was doing in Tokyo, about his work in movies, and shop talk in general. As the conversation began building in ease and fluency, they talked about Vince's hopes and dreams and plans when he came out to Hollywood.

"I told him, too, about the struggles I'd been having, and my discouragements," Vince recalled. "Then Welles gave me some advice I've never forgotten."

Welles, who listened sympathetically to the young actor across from him, perhaps thought of his own disillusions as he said with deadly seriousness: "Vince, nothing in this world, is just handed to a guy. You must go after it. You say the breaks are bad sometimes. Well, sure they are. But have you ever thought of making your own breaks?

"I did that for years. Sometimes you don't get a break. Sometimes it's so bad you come up with a compound fracture. Well, okay, that's supposed to be a joke. But still, you try, you always have a chance.

"It's the old adage, God helps those who help themselves. Remember that. It's important. And try to forgive for rattling on like an old sage of the desert or something. God knows I've made my share of mistakes.

"But I also made my breaks."

Intrigued by the Japanese way of life, Vince decided to stay on in Tokyo a while longer rather than see the rest of Japan. The days became weeks and the weeks months and Vince still had no word from his studio. He'd expected another assignment, a better one this time, within a few weeks at the most.

Now, with some trepidation and vaguely afraid of the answer he'd receive, the restless actor decided to cable the studio. The answer was as prompt as it was crushing. The studio had no plans for him for the immediate future, the reply said, but of course if anything came up they would call him.

Vince stuffed the wire angrily into his pocket and strode off into the streets of Tokyo, muttering out loud to himself.

"They'll call me. Ha! What a laugh. Don't call me, I'll call you," he snapped bitterly.

"But that's quite impossible, I do not do business that way," a small, bell-like voice suddenly rang out.

It startled Vince. He spun around. At his elbow was a young woman. She gave him a puzzled look. He returned it.

"What?" he asked in bewilderment. "Are you talking to me?"

"Of course. Weren't you talking to me? Didn't you say not to call you?"

"Well . . . yes, but I wasn't . . ."

Vince stopped speechless. How did he get involved in this farce?

The girl spoke.

"These pictures I take will be delivered to you only if you wish to fill out one of these cards with your name and address."

Then he saw the camera she was carrying and suddenly it began to make sense.

"You mean you're one of those street photographers like we have Stateside?"

No, sir, she replied I do not take pictures of the streets. Only of people and they will cost you, for one, fifty cents, American money."

When Vince remembers the scene now he laughs.

"I looked down and saw a doll," he says. "She was tiny, just like most Japanese women, but she didn't have the real Oriental slant to her eyes. She was slightly Americanized, even in her dress, and her English was flawless."

And that was the start of Vince Edwards' long and haunting interlude with Michiko.

Michiko was then going to college and was helping to pay for her tuition by working for her father, who owned a photography shop in Tokyo. She took pictures of tourists in the street, and at night occasionally filled in as "camera girl" at Takachiko's Golden Hours, one of the better nightspots and, she hurried to assure Vince, "very proper and of very good repute."

Vince and Michiko began seeing more and more of each other. By day, when she wasn't in classes, he'd accompany her on her photographic rounds of Tokyo's winding, busy streets, sometimes joining with her in persuading a particularly reluctant tourist to stand still and watch the birdie. Daily, there would be cozy lunches in dimly lit restaurants, walks through the park, bicycle rides to the countryside, surf swimming in the warm Pacific, all of the million and one things a guy and a girl do together.

By night, there'd be dancing in night clubs, long walks later in the cool darkness outside, quiet private dinners at her home. Each became lost in one another's presence—and inevitably, according to Vince himself, they fell in love.

Michiko doted on Vince. As he recalled later, "Their way is so different from ours. A woman is born and raised for one purpose, to satisfy and please her man. I must confess I loved it. In fact, I was getting spoiled by that kind of treatment."

Today, Vince is a little reluctant to talk of his romance with Michiko. He'll tell of some of the lighter moments they shared, but little else.

One anecdote he's fond of relating was of the time they dropped into a supper club that proudly advertised "American-Type Orchestra." "

"I burst out laughing when the master of ceremonies came on stage and said, 'And now we play that latest hit from America, "You Can Depend on Me," sung by the Japanese Pat Boone, Taki Kuroso.'

"The band got off to a horrible start and I kept laughing, and Michiko asked me what was so funny. I told her that the song wasn't the latest hit at all and that Pat Boone was getting a lot more attention lately for his acting rather than his singing, and that certainly the little five-foot-tall guy in the blue tux and white shoes up there croaking the lyrics sounded about as much like Pat Boone as Ed Sullivan did.

"Then Michiko turns to me with a puzzled look and says, 'I thought Ed Sullivan was a newspaperman, not a singer.'

"And I said, 'Michiko, honey, it looks like that business of *never the twain shall meet* is true.' "

It was said in jocular good humor at the time, but the remark held within it the seed of a truth that later both would come to regret and then hate but finally, painfully, acknowledge and accept.

It soon became clear to Vince that they couldn't go on as they were.

"It was like something out of *Madame Butterfly*," he remembers. "I knew she wouldn't be happy in the States and I couldn't stay in her land forever. We reached a point where some decision had to be made."

But knowing the decision must be made didn't make it any easier. Their lives were tightly entwined by love.

It was then that Vince Edwards came closest to ending his career as an actor. He had all but convinced himself that his love for Michiko was more powerful than all his plans and dreams and hopes to be an actor. And yet he knew a man's worth is measured by the work he does in his lifetime and that a man must be true to himself, and at some critical moment in that terrible time of indecision Orson Welles' words came back to him . . . ". . . nothing in this world is handed a guy . . . you have to go after it . . . have you ever thought of making your own breaks . . ."

Vince knew what his decision had to be.

Helping him make that decision was a cable from Hollywood, It was from John Cassavetes, his old friend.

"Have fine part for you in *Too Late Blues*. Bobby Darin to star. Great opportunity. Come back at once."

Vince Edwards made up his mind—he was going back!

Michiko hid her grief. In a drizzling rain at the airport, she fought back the tears as Vince held her in his arms. Softly, as she lifted her lips to his, they kissed.

"I can never forget you," she whispered.

Vince turned and walked toward the plane, a small figure vanishing into the night.

For a long while afterwards, his friends say, Vince wasn't the same. He threw himself furiously into his career, but often, at nights in a restaurant, or gazing out the window of his home, he'd fall into deep melancholy silences, letting his mind drift across the broad breast of the heaving Pacific.

It was goodbye to Michiko—but not forever. For Vince one day would again see her when he finally reached the mighty heights of Dr. Ben Casey.

But for the moment, it would seem that the ever-moving tides of life had washed away the past forever, despite the soldiers' sad ballad . . .

. . . East is East and West is West, our worlds are far apart. I must leave you now, but I leave my heart.

8
"MEDIC" AND THE PRIVATE EYES

JOHN CASSAVETES wanted Vincent Edwards because there was no one like him—an actor without airs and graces; he was always the same man, the man who played the mobster and the killer in a score of films, the man who played Mr. Universe because he had the muscle and brawn for such a role. An all-around actor with vast experience, training—and talent.

His brooding looks, his angry disposition, his rugged physical appearance lent themselves to the character Cassavetes envisioned for *Too Late Blues*. He wanted someone to play a psychopathic bigot—and John couldn't think of anyone more suited for that role than Vincent Edwards.

But *Too Late Blues* was not Vince Edwards' vehicle to impress the critics. His part was small and the character he played, Tommy, barely made the cast list. Movie reviewers who gave the film a lukewarm reception at best, failed to find anything to say about Vince.

After this picture, Vince looked around disheartenedly for more work. He finally found it in television. He was still the heavy—always either stealing the hero's girl or murdering somebody.

But even with video's increasing popularity and the vastly greater number of jobs opened to actors and entertainers who once depended on Hollywood films for a living. Vince still encountered long stretches of unemployment. As 1960 neared a close, Vince looked around in desperation.

Suddenly he decided he'd try something he'd always wanted to do—sing.

"It wasn't exactly in desperation," Vince says. "It was what they were doing and it seemed like the right thing for me."

Opportunity to cut a record beckoned. Capitol signed Vince to do "Lollipop" and "Widget."

"We were the first with it," Vince recalls, "but we were well covered. The Chordettes had the big hit. My record made a little noise and we sold a few discs. But let's just say they released it and that was it. My option wasn't picked up."

On July 7, 1960, Vince's heart was grieved by a telegram from home, a message from his mother.

"DAD DIED TODAY. HE PASSED AWAY IN HOSPITAL . . ."

The family had been expecting it. For nearly a year, Papa Vincent had suffered from lung cancer. The end came in Brooklyn's Lutheran Hospital.

Vincent flew home for the funeral, then returned immediately to the Coast.

As Vince fell into another deep chasm of depression, the fates that had been toying with his life elevator-like, lifting and dropping him, finally took him on another climb. This time it was a call to do a television portrayal of a frontier doctor on *The Deputy* weekly series.

Vince was superb in his role. He did not don white coat and mask. He did not wield scalpel. He didn't call for sutures. He simply played a frontier physician on horseback.

Among those who became cognizant of Vince's excellent portrayal in *The Deputy* was Abby Greshler, a Hollywood agent who had brought along stars like Dean Martin and Jerry Lewis. Greshler didn't represent Vince nor did he know the actor. He only knew that Vince's acting in that particular TV production was top-grade. He also had seen Vince in some of his movies.

Greshler did nothing at the moment to promote Edwards, since there was no reason for the agent to do so. His job is finding and providing talent for the studios or television producers who ask for it. Since he was not representing Edwards, he was not going to go out of his way to make any connections for him.

Nevertheless, Greshler would soon play a significant in Vince Edwards' career.

Leading up to the critical turn in Vince's career was a series of events which began with television producer James Moser. He was the man who literally pioneered bringing the medical profession to the TV screen with the show called *Medic*.

Medic had had its run on the cathode tube and was in the early part of 1961, a mere headstone in the vast graveyard of defunct television series and shows. It had died in comparative infancy despite the fact that it had started out its video life in robust health. Its popularity waned, and when that happens it is no different than a human being who contracts a terminal illness.

Death can't be cheated.

Medic had been interred for some years, but there were bales of material which had been dug up by Moser's research staff and never used. The material was kept in files.

One day, Moser was walking through the corridor of Los Angeles General Hospital. As he passed a surgeon's office, he heard the doctor blowing off at a patient on the phone. This doctor had no bedside manner in his conversation, Moser concluded. He also wondered. Is that the way a doctor really is? Why not? A doctor is busy. He is involved in life and death day in and day out. He has no time for social amenities. He has his work. Why shouldn't a doctor be angry, surly, curt, caustic, rude, and bad-tempered?

140

"That's it!" Moser told himself. "An angry but dedicated doctor—to play in a new television series!"

Eagerly, he went to Bing Crosby Productions, one of Groaner's multi-tentacled business enterprises which was recently created to produce video shows. It had yet to produce its first.

He broached the idea of a medical series—a series starring a neurosurgeon. Crosby's outfit liked it, decided to invest capital in a pilot film, which is designed as the forerunner of a series. It's the one shown to the TV networks and to sponsors. If they like this initial show, they contract for it on an annual basis.

Moser and Howard Koch of Bing Crosby Productions, agreed the show should be an hour long. They would name it *Ben Casey* after its central character.

There was one hitch.

Who would play the angry but dedicated neurosurgeon?

The man would have to be ruggedly handsome and overpoweringly appealing.

"Get me such a man," Moser ordered his casting director.

Days and weeks passed. Sixty candidates were screen-tested for the role. All sixty were rejected.

The chief complaint against most of them was that they were too effeminate. That's probably symptomatic of today's trend in Hollywood and television—too many pretty boys. Not enough Clark Gable and Gary Cooper types.

One day, out of desperation, Koch decided to make a stab himself at landing an actor to play Ben Casey. He phoned Abby Greshler, the agent.

"We're trying frantically to find a Ben Casey," Koch told Greshler. "We've gone through sixty guys, but they're all too silk-stockinged, or they just don't fit the role. Can you recommend someone we could try?"

Greshler is a hep guy. But the request left him slightly in the dark.

"What's a Ben Casey?" he prodded with justifiable innocence.

"Oh," Koch came back. "I should have told you . . ." And he proceeded to explain.

"I think I might be able to solve your problem," Greshler offered. "There's an actor who's been kicking around town for years. He's done a lot of gangster stuff for Columbia and some of the other studios, and I remember him playing a rugged doctor on *The Deputy* series not long ago. His. name's Vincent Edwards."

"How do I get in touch with him?" Koch asked.

"I don't know," Greshler replied. "I don't handle him. But I think I can contact him. Meanwhile, I suggest you look at some of his films."

Koch immediately summoned Moser and producer Matthew Rapf. They sent for Edwards' films. They viewed them. They watched with intense interest the anger, the surliness, the curtness, the rudeness, the bad temper that Vince had to employ in his gangster roles. They envisioned him in the white coat of a neurosurgeon. They tried to see Vince with a white surgical mask over his face. They studied his eyes. They were deep, intense, reflective.

They liked what they saw.

Most of all they liked him because he looked rugged and muscular. He was tall and filled out. And he was handsome.

He was the original angry man—a perfect prototype for the angry Dr. Ben Casey.

"Let's get him!" Moser exclaimed.

Koch phoned Greshler.

"We like Edwards," he said. "We'd like him to come over and take a test. Have you found him?"

Greshler had already started his search, but it had led nowhere. He hadn't been able to find Vince. He had somehow mysteriously disappeared.

"Don't worry," Greshler promised. "I'll get him if I have to hire the entire Los Angeles Police Department."

He almost had to.

At least he had to retain crack Hollywood private detectives to take part in the trackdown.

The private eyes checked nightclubs, Malibu Beach, glues of starlets, Schwab's—anywhere that Vince was known to hang out. Nothing.

Then they tried Santa Anita, keeping an eye on the pari-mutuel windows where Vince was known to make brief stopovers. Nothing.

Then one day a detective returned to Malibu Beach and came upon a motorcycle race. One rider seemed familiar. The detective took a look at Vince Edwards' mug shot he was carrying.

"That's him," the shamus said.

But how could he stop a guy scooting along on a motorcycle at sixty?

The detective inquired. He learned that Edwards had won the race and gone off to a friend's place. The sleuth tracked down Vince finally—under the friend's racing car.

"I found him under the car, making repairs," the detective reported to Greshler in triumph. "I guess he likes cars, too."

Vince was ordered to report to the Desilu Studios for tests. He passed those like a thoroughbred. He was in!

Next came work on the pilot. A script was plunked into Vince's hands.

"Study it, learn it, and come back in a week," he was directed.

Then came the shooting.

"Tremendous!" rejoiced Moser after viewing the finished pilot. "We won't have any trouble with this."

And they didn't. The American Broadcasting Company took one look and decided they'd buy the series.

And that's how a mountain of old medical research that was good for nothing, suddenly became good for something.

It took a character like Ben Casey to bring it back to life.

And it took a character like Vincent Edwards to bring Ben Casey to life.

9
DR. BEN CASEY GOES ON TV

"AFTER JIM MOSER interviewed me," Vince Edwards says, "I was pretty certain he liked me . . . I gathered that I would get the part of Ben Casey. I didn't know what I was getting into, but I had a feeling it was a terrific opportunity."

Not Vince, not Moser, not Greshler, not Rapf, not Crosby—not anyone—really knew what they were getting into. They could only hope and pray that the vast American television audiences would receive the show as a welcome change from the ferocious violence battering their sensibilities day in and day out in the guise of Westerns and gangster shows.

Already protests over TV blood and thunder had reached such proportions that a Congressional committee was prompted to conduct a full-scale investigation into the comportment of TV shows.

As the seismic eruptions over the gory TV programs were raging, *Ben Casey* came on the air in October, 1961.

But before the show premiered, there were many hectic months of preparation. And before the preparations there had to be a working arrangement with the star of the show—a contract and agreement on salary.

147

Abby Greshler learned Vince had no agent for the moment and took him under his wing.

"We'll get a good price, Vince," promised Greshler with the confidence that only a Hollywood agent can mount.

Abby huddled and haggled with Moser and the big wigs at Bing Crosby Productions until they struck the "price"—$1,750 a week! This was a salary scale that was astronomical for Vince. Six times more than he'd ever made in his whole nondescript actor's career. He was understandably exultant.

To add to Vince's security and confidence, they gave him a three-year contract. It was a better deal than either he or Greshler had secretly hoped for.

Then came the selection of the rest of the cast.

Although there was considerable originality in the mold Moser shaped for his show, he did adapt a number of ideas from the movies' famed Dr. Kildare series which dominated the nation's screens in the decade between 1938 and 1948. Moviegoers may recall that Lew Ayres played the title role while the late Lionel Barrymore was the elder Dr. Gillespie.

Significantly, as *Ben Casey* was being rapidly fashioned into shape, the National Broadcasting Company was preparing a medical series of its own—the famed Dr. Kildare show. Richard Chamberlain, a tall, handsome, blond twenty-six-year-old little-known actor was selected for the lead and veteran Raymond Massey for the role of Dr. Gillespie.

In his format, Moser created Dr. David Zorba, a so-called "doctor-patron" who would guide and "ride" Dr. Casey over the rough spots of his internship, a Dr. Gillespie of sorts. For the part, Moser sought veteran Broadway-Hollywood actor Sam Jaffe. At 63, Jaffe had gone the full gamut of the entertainment world as linguist, pianist, composer, as well as thespian of the stage and screen. Jaffe starred on Broadway in *Grand Hotel*—and that was back in 1930. His career started long before then.

A profound innovation in television medical annals was installed in *Ben Casey* by the inclusion of a woman physician, Dr. Maggie Graham. Director Fielder Cook had the type in mind, but he didn't have the type in hand. He found her, however—quite by chance.

Sam Jaffe had come to Hollywood for a costume fitting for the pilot film of *Ben Casey*, accompanied by youthful actress Bettye Ackerman, who in private life is Sam's wife. She had just finished her first movie, *Face of Fire*, after a distinctive career on the Broadway stage.

Bettye was waiting for Sam when director Cook walked up to her with a script.

"Bettye," he said casually, "Would you please read for the part of Dr. Graham."

Wearing work shirt and blue jeans as she was, Bettye begged off.

"Perhaps another time when I'm dressed," she smiled. I would rather not do it now."

Cook was insistent. Bettye acceded, and read.

"You're it!" Cook announced jubilantly.

Then came the other featured players—Harry Landers, as Dr. Ted Hoffman; Barton Heyman as Dr. Paul Cain, an intern, and Jeanne Bates, as a nurse.

Next came rehearsals. The set chosen for this document was huge Sound Stage Twelve of Desilu Studios where many major TV series had been filmed. But the set for *Ben Casey* required additional facilities, and these were found at Los Angeles General Hospital.

The basic story line was woven around the lives of a group of neurosurgeons; as in Dr. Kildare the story's central character was a young intern, Dr. Casey.

As creator of the series, Moser took a direct and firm hand in the production. Not only did he provide the ideas and ride herd on the writing of the script, but he also took an active part ironing out the multitude of technical difficulties that kept rising to the surface during preparation of the show.

For one thing, this was a series that dealt with a highly delicate subject—medicine. It could not be presented any other way except realistically and accurately. To ensure that it was, professional guidance was mandatory.

As a one-time San Francisco newspaperman, Moser knew the importance of accuracy and realism. He had had experience on that need when he was doing *Medic* back in 1954, 1955, and 1956. And he had also learned that need earlier when he wrote scripts for Dr. Kildare movies—while, at the same time, incidentally, doing the scripts for Jack Webb's radio *Dragnet* series.

So, to assure authenticity, he sought out the advice and aid of the American Medical Association. The AMA was happy to assist in guiding the producers, directors, and cast in hospital procedures as well as medical and surgical techniques.

The show was designed to establish from the outset the image of Dr. Ben Casey as a hardened-artery guy, a medical bully who runs roughshod over fellow physicians and drives nurses back to mother. Working for $65 a week, Casey must live in the hospital, work around the clock, never sleep, and be able to handle any case from maternity to brain surgery.

Vince Edwards sized up his role in this way: "Right from the beginning, I saw Ben Casey as a moody fellow, somewhat withdrawn yet always moved by a sense of devotion to his work which he regards as a high calling.

"There was a big cry for public service films. Stories that would inspire youth. Ben is that kind of person. He's no appeaser. He's on the verge of dismissal, but is considered the finest resident in twenty-one years.

"This was not intended to be a soap opera, and never will so long as I play Casey. There are no cliches and no trite situations. Ben is an intense man fighting death—but he won't always win out. Sometimes the patient will die.

"But he's obsessed with the fight—like Eliot Ness is with crime."

His dedication was contagious. It seemed to be inherent in the aims and aspirations of Moser, Edwards, Jaffe, Ackerman, and the rest who would be the practitioners of the medical arts banded together in the incessant, relentless war against the ills and infirmities plaguing mankind.

Realism had to be a keynote. In fact, Moser had become so infatuated, perhaps obsessed, with medicine that his desire to bring fidelity to the cathode tube was awash with innuendos and suspicions that he wanted every TV set to reek of ether every Monday night from 10 to 11 P.M.

The setting for the filmed series was a mythical County General Hospital in an unnamed metropolis. It could be New York or Chicago or Boston or San Francisco or Los Angeles.

Few weekly series are without a love interest and, in that respect, Ben Casey was no different. Therefore Dr. Casey was billeted for romantic peregrinations with pretty Dr. Maggie Graham, whose role on the hospital staff is an anesthesiologist. But after a hot start, Moser limited the hearts and flowers bit to a bare minimum, in the belief that the stories would bear more credence.

Occasionally, Vince and Bettye may touch each other's hand while sipping coffee or talking over a case, but that's the limit. It was a basic taboo from the inception of *Ben Casey* for doctors to go around pinching nurses.

In the first film and some succeeding ones, Ben and Maggie went in for strong love scenes.

"But we realized we couldn't keep the romance at that level," Bettye reflected recently when the subject of a waning romance with Ben came up. "There was no place to go except a marriage ceremony."

So the torrid romance was put under wraps. Dr. Graham was told to show more interest to her oxygen tanks and Dr. Casey to his scalpel and sutures.

All did not go perfectly smooth in the preparation and filming of the first *Ben Casey* show. There were many among the production's executives who

153

were concerned with the effect Sam Jaffe's somewhat limited role would have on viewing audiences familiar with his acting talents. The script confined Jaffe's part as Dr. Zorba largely to the role of watchdog over the impetuous and tactless Dr. Casey, getting him out of jams, and putting him in his place by saying, "Sorry, Ben, I have no choice but to overrule your decision—I am discharging your patient."

But Jaffe was not disturbed in the least that he was not given a chance to flex his acting muscles as one of most respected and versatile performers in the American theater.

"I play the role that is given me and I give it my best," Jaffe said. "After all, this is a story about Ben Casey, not David Zorba. Put the spotlight on Casey and let's get on with the show."

And the show went on. "

The early rushes viewed in the projection room gave Moser and company extreme satisfaction with the way the cast performed. Vince was sensational in his brooding, snarling, angry way.

"The women will flip over. him the way they flipped over Gable thirty years ago," Moser enthused.

The gaunt, graying Moser's dedication to the medical profession engendered itself in an unswerving policy of technical perfection. Every scene had to be flawless. To help perfect each scene, Moser induced a friend, Dr. Allan M. Warner, to leave his position as chief resident in neurosurgery at Los Angeles County General Hospital and become technical adviser for the series.

Dr. Warner's contributions were put into use at once. He took the scripts and fine-tooth-combed them for accuracy and proper application of medical procedures, as well as the correct use of terminology.

Beyond that, Moser set down in writing what the basic purpose and mold of the show must be. He prepared a "story guide" and directed his writers to read it and follow its rules. In the guide, he says, in part: "*Ben Casey* is NOT *Medic*. We are not doing a series of medical case histories. We do not intend to become as clinically involved as was generally the case in *Medic*.

"On the other hand, we do not intend to do a soap opera set against a hospital background. We do not want stories which, with a few pencil changes, could just as easily become a Western or an adventure mystery.

"*Ben Casey* is primarily a series of adult, honest-to-God stories about people in medicine—specifically, young doctors in training. Let's keep it that way.

"These stories will deal first and foremost with our principal characters, their problems, both personal and professional, their patients, their day-to-day living in a 4,000-bed medical arena that is packed with emotion, action, laughter, and tragedy—and above all and always, important human problems.

"We must take a fair but scrupulously honest look at these men of medicine in training; at the older professional men who have gone before them, and the younger men who will soon follow in their stead."

Production moved along swiftly and by the time the last weekend before the premiere had rolled around, the entire company associated with *Ben Casey* began to breathe easier. They had completed three shows and were well on their way into the fourth. Now all that they were concerned with was the premiere—the all-important "opening night."

What would the critics say?

How would the nation's television viewers receive the show?

The answers came soon after that all-critical moment when *Ben Casey* had completed its first full-hour's run over the ABC network on the night of Monday, October 3, 1961.

The reaction came first from the nation's TV critics. Here is how the columnists who can make or break a show reacted:

Ben Gross of the *New York Daily News*—

"... *Ben Casey* ... is a rough and tough sample of medical drama. It has 'realistic' touches but is played in such an abrasive style that one wondered whether he had tuned in *The Untouchables* by mistake . . . Vincent Edwards portrays the surly Dr. Casey and Sam Jaffe plays Edwards' superior with an amazing abandon."

Percy Shain, *Boston Globe*—

"It isn't hard to spot the newest idol of two important and overlapping segments of the TV viewing audience—the women and the young folks.

"He's 31-year-old [actually 33 by now] Vincent Edwards, the darkly handsome, rugged hero of *Ben Casey*, the new ABC series seen Monday nights on Channel 7. By all odds, Vince has made the greatest impact hereabouts of all the 'unknowns' pushed into stardom in the precipitous way that TV has chosen to adopt."

William Peper, *New York World-Telegram & Sun*—

"The title character, played by Vincent Edwards, is a surly young doctor who thinks he is one of the few intelligent persons in an outfit full of fools and frauds, a not common delusion in any business.

"He is exposed to rabies but is allergic to the vaccines that cure the fatal disease. He may have only thirty days to live. Since he is the title character in a show that is scheduled to run all season, it's a little hard to work up any anxiety about his chances of dying on opening night."

Lawrence Laurent, *Washington Post*—

"*Ben Casey* is a sort of hospital troublemaker. He keeps hospital executives in a sweat over the way he practices medicine. His bedside manner is reminiscent of the way a bear reacts to being awakened from hibernation. Yet the strength of the writing and the strength of the leading players is so great that *Ben Casey* is probably the best serious filmed drama on television . . .

"Edwards is ruggedly handsome, without the sticky, feminine prettiness of the television heroes in such shows as *Surfside Six, Adventures in Paradise,* and *Hawaiian Eye*. He . . . seems determined to prove that medicine is a profession for those who like long hours and low pay."

Variety—

". . . Preachy and overdone, the first *Ben Casey* did, however, smack of authenticity—at times— which suggests that once the bugs are out of the way, it'll settle down into a more satisfyingly realistic groove . . .

"Edwards, a fine actor who has learned the film trade by appearing mainly as offbeat criminal types in B features, performed erratically during the first half hour of *Casey* but his laconic behavior became steadier and more meaningful as the program progressed . . .

"Show's chances are, at least, middling good to grab a durable notch for itself in nighttime TV."

Jack O'Brian, *New York Journal-American*—
". . . it's another grim one, if not so surgically stark and unyielding in its wallop as *Medic*.

"It's intentionally tough, though, with a rough and naturally brilliant young neurosurgeon as its hero, played by Vincent Edwards on a one-note of humorless urgency, as if he had only to the finish of the show to perform a great operation and die. He almost did die, from drowning in the plot as two counterplots whirlpooled their talents last night, one about an endearing small boy whose skull Dr. Ben was waiting to excavate, the other a possible attack of rabies which could have done Dr. Casey in before even an option dropped. Because the show was sold for the whole season, it seemed unlikely they'd kill off the young genius last night, so the tension didn't quite mount . . .

". . . it seems the villain of this weekly piece is Dr. Ben's own personality—abrasive, even a bit ugly, not so much a bedside manner as jailside. He's rough and uncouth but simply awash with genius, impatient of the shortcomings of ordinary doctors, ragged-edging the nerve ends of the hospital board, frustratingly bothersome to his old doctor-patron, played by Sam Jaffe more like crusty shopkeeper than a doctor.

"It's a *Dr. Kildare* series without the sugar and spice or anything nice . . ."

Jack Gould, *The New York Times*—

"He [Edwards] excoriates a young assistant, reducing him to tears, and then wheels a dying patient down hospital corridors in the wildest vehicular sprint since *Ben Hur*. He attempts to save the patient's life. The process is a vigorous one, including sharp blows to the chest, but the patient dies.

". . . He may know his scalpels and sutures, but there is a calculated element of shock in the new series that is extreme and unnecessary. Dr. Casey needs a quick tranquilizer.

Perhaps Vince Edwards was intolerant of sham, angry and impatient with the world, and anxious to do what he could to minister to the needs of the sick and the dying. He snapped and snarled at the world that night from the cathode tube and thirty-two million TV sets vibrated as Vince sprinted through the hospital corridors like a knight sterile surgical armor.

It was too soon to know after the final scene of that opening show what impact Vince Edwards made on the vast nationwide audience. But it wouldn't be long before everyone would know.

As Ben Casey, he had created an imposing image on TV, so powerful and immense that uncounted millions were to look upon Vincent Edwards in the weeks ahead as a dynamic personality—a hulking, slab-shouldered man who was on his way to becoming the entertainment world's brightest new star.

10
THE BIG TIME

FOR A DOZEN long, dreary years Hollywood had virtually ignored Vince Edwards. He was the actor nobody wanted. Then suddenly he became an overnight star, a struggling reject sensationally rocketed into a show-business phenomenon in a television show fated for outstanding success from the first spinal tap.

Vince himself was elated by the show's enormous reception, but he was overwhelmed by the tidal wave of popularity that surged over him personally. The struggling reject was suddenly a glittering star in the television heavens as women from six to sixty flip-flapped over the rugged, angrily brooding neurosurgeon.

Letters from the fans—the most accurate barometer of appreciation—poured in at the rate of five hundred the first week, a thousand the second, fifteen hundred the third, and from then on at that same clip week in and week out. The females of 1961-1962 proved to be no different from the females of the 1920's who wrote to Rudolph Valentino and of the 1930's to Clark Gable. Letters by the bushel were carted into the studio bearing one traditional central theme—proposals of marriage, the most complimentary tribute a fan can pay a star.

During an interview with Richard K. Shull of the *Indianapolis Times*, Vince was asked what big change had taken place in his life since *Ben Casey* went on the air.

"Well," replied the actor with typical candor, "everybody in town with a cracked head calls me. And I'm getting a lot of phone calls from strangers—giggling females. And lots of fan mail."

Then Shull asked how things were with Sam Jaffe.

"Oh," Vince said in all seriousness, "he took the week off. He's in Chicago addressing a medical convention . . . He was invited to speak, so he prepared a half-hour speech and took off."

Vince also was called upon to tour the so-called "banquet circuit," speaking to Parent-Teacher Associations, nurses' groups, and performing at benefits of all types. His free time was not his own anymore.

As for work, it was all that and more. From dawn to dusk or, as Edwards puts it, "from dark to dark," he was at the studio reading the seventy pages of script to be memorized each week along with numerous and difficult medical terminologies, and rehearsal and, finally, performing before the cameras and lights.

As the show snowballed into a smashing success, boiling the Neilsen ratings up to astronomic highs,

Edwards' services came into insistent demand beyond the TV studio confines. To get an idea of how big Vince Edwards became in the brief space of a few months, listen to his agent, Abby Greshler:

"I knew I had a star on my hands when people began to ring my phone incessantly, particularly people from whom I hadn't heard in years. Suddenly they were buddy-buddy as if we had been dealing with each other all along.

"They wanted Vince for every conceivable idea you could imagine—charity shows, fashion soirees, telethons. Even movies—major studios were calling, asking if he were available for starring roles.

"That didn't end there. Recording companies and nightclubs, knowing Vince has a voice and had turned out a few platters, were after him.

"TV shows, too, like the *Dinah Shore* and *Garry Moore* and *Perry Como Shows* besieged him with offers through me.

"I knew I had a big star but I also knew that I had to watch his exposure and also watch out for the big money, which is my job.

"The way I look at it, Vince can wind up with between three and four million dollars—free and clear—in the next three or four years. And that isn't bad."

When Greshler spoke of that kind of money, he had in mind earnings Vince would make after he had formed one or two of his own corporations, the way most of today's stars are doing. Stars who haven't done this, and are still on straight salary, are lucky to end up with one-tenth of their earnings in any given period. Uncle Sam's Internal Revenue Service gobbles up the rest with a ravenous appetite.

"This boy," said Greshler, "is big business now—very big business. And I think he'll go right on being big business—maybe ten to fifteen years, barring death or accidents."

Even as Greshler spoke, he was hiring people to count Vince Edwards' piles of gold pouring in from ancillary enterprises that suddenly sprung up in deference to his new star status. One of the biggest sources of "side" money cascaded in from the manufacture and sale of Ben Casey merchandise——objects like button-down-the-side intern-style shirts. In less than six months the sale of Ben Casey merchandise reached five and a half million dollars and the outlook was for twenty-five million dollars in total retail sales!

Vince Edwards, as Ben Casey, not only became the rage in novelty merchandise, but had women's blouses and shirts named after him. Even the fashion industry was influenced by the Casey craze. During the summer of 1962, one of the leading

Paris designers came out with a Ben Casey blouse for women!

There was an offer also from London, from producer-director Carl Foreman, who had once turned down Vince for a part in his Academy Award-winning film *High Noon*. Foreman wanted Vince for a lead role in *The Victors*, which he planned to shoot in late summer of 1962.

The film was to have an imposing cast, including Oscar-winner Sophia Loren; George Peppard, who starred in *Breakfast at Tiffany's* with Audrey Hepburn, and George Hamilton, star of *Light in the Piazza* with Yvette Mimieux.

Vince didn't have to be asked twice. He knew this was his golden opportunity. He wanted the part; and the part for him was that of an American GI named Baker, who is teased and tormented by his fellow soldiers because he refuses to take advantage of the hungry girls in war-torn Italy.

The girl who wins his sympathy was to be Miss Loren, the script called for love scenes that would be tender, restrained, and quietly dignified.

Vince and Abby Greshler didn't need much time to decide.

"Cable my acceptance," Vince advised his agent.

The salary for the stint, which was to take a month of his time, amounted to $100,000, not bad for four weeks' work.

Other good offers came along, but Vince was too deeply involved with *Ben Casey* to take them. He was able to commit himself to *The Victors* only because it would be during the last half of August and first half of September, when the *Casey* cast was on vacation.

Vince, however, did accept one of the more lucrative offers—from the *Dinah Shore Show*. It was a $10,000 guest star appearance, and the fact that the show as on the rival National Broadcasting Company made not an iota of difference. It's in Vince's contract with Crosby and ABC that he can appear on any other network, provided it doesn't conflict with his duties in *Ben Casey*.

Goin on Dinah's show was a stirring change from his weekly routine on the medical program. Vince drove a nationwide audience into a figurative tizzy when he came on stage sans scalpel and stethoscope and promptly plunged into a song and dance routine. The teenagers in the audience squealed in delirium. The next day columnists who hadn't known of his background as a singer, wrote great gobs of praise as if Vince had just acquired his musical talents overnight. Few knew the years of his struggle, the lessons paid for by Mama Julie, the heartbreaks he endured.

If they didn't know it before, Bing and ABC knew it then—they had a big thing on their hands, a sort of national craze, like The Twist. An instant legend!

During a hiatus in filming, ABC summoned Vince to Chicago to appear on a show staged by the network for representatives of its affiliate stations attending the National Association of Broadcasters convention. When Vince arrived in the Windy City, he was handled like a hothouse bloom by the network's publicity people, the "flacks" as they're called.

In their obsession to shield him from fanatical fans who whip into a frenzied rendition of the screaming meamies whenever they set eyes on Vince, the flacks shielded Vince with all the privacy accorded a head of state on a secret diplomatic mission.

Vince arrived in Chicago by train, was met by the network's people, and whisked to the Conrad Hilton for the show in the International Ballroom. All during this time, he was accorded the full VIP treatment reserved for movie stars of the first magnitude.

This sort of adulation for Vince, coupled with the hero worship which inevitably fell at his feet, could send a guy's ego spiraling into a disastrous orbit if he isn't smart enough to sense the pitfalls. Vince didn't want success to go to his head—he forced himself to think back to the hard times and hard knocks he encountered on his way up.

"I was prepared mentally," Vince said. "I knew the show had it and that something had to happen. And it did. Not all, but some of my old friends began to weigh their words when we got together. They still do. 'They don't see me as plain old Vince Edwards. What they see now is 'The Image.' They see Ben Casey. It makes a difference, believe me. Their attitudes change. They stiffen. I can't say I like that.

"And I'm not so sure I like losing a little privacy. I wish it were different, in some ways, the whole success thing. But that's how it is and how do you fight it?"

The struggling reject-turned-success didn't fight the sudden good times he came upon.

One day out of the blue a black Lincoln-Continental slithered gracefully, as only a Lincoln-Continental can slither, into the Desilu lot and pulled up in front of Sound Stage Twelve. The man behind the wheel, obviously a chauffeur, jumped out and hurried around to open the door for the passenger in the back—Vince Edwards.

It was quite a change, this sleek $12,000 luxury car, from the old beat-up jalopy Vince had been barreling around in before the gods of show business blessed him with their kindness and generosity.

"A few months ago when Vince started to work on the *Ben Casey* series, he was meek as a lamb, drove a battered and dented 1958 Ford, and his dressing room was a mere cubbyhole in a dark corner of the stage. Not only that but he was thousands of dollars in debt—a hangover from his sporadic success in finding jobs in the acting field during the past twelve years."

Speaking was Carroll Nye, one of Big Crosby Productions executives.

Now, Vince had the 1962 Continental and a chauffeur with it. The chauffeur was Benny Goldberg, a former lightweight fighter and long-time friend of Vince. Benny didn't wear a chauffeur's uniform, but merely a sports outfit that consisted of a red shirt, blue trousers, and loud blue and white checkered jacket. Sometimes the color motif was blue. Other times beige. But always, Benny looked as dapper as a movie star, Benny with the small beady eyes and squashed nose that was a monument to the days of old when he was a pug on the circuit.

Benny's salary was a neat $250 a week, paid for by Bing Crosby Productions at Vince's request. Benny's other duties beside driving Vince around include being a "gofor" boy—he goes for coffee and cigarettes and tends to many of Vince's business dealings.

As for Vince, as he enters the sound stage now, he no longer goes to the hole-in-the-wall dressing room but, rather, to a splendid private suite of dressing rooms, the plushest to be found anywhere in Hollywood. Vince Edwards' name is on the door. Outside, next to the door is a telephone with a large sign proclaiming, "Mr. Edwards' private telephone."

Vince and Benny enter, the later opens the dressing room door for his boss, then takes a seat at a desk outside by the phone. This is Benny's desk where he holds court with visitors who want to see Vince. Needless to say, no one can get in without first being "screened" by Benny. And it goes without saying that no one not wanted is going to get by, not with Benny around, Benny who is a past master in the manly art of self-defense—and offense.

Inside, the dressing room is painted a pleasant pastel green and off-white. There are two private phones, a portable TV set with remote dialing controls, stereophonic record player, not to mention the exquisite furnishings in Danish modern. Moreover, one room has a bed so the star can take naps if he desires; another room is a Pullman kitchen of sorts, with a small refrigerator and other convenient utilities.

It should be pointed out that the dressing room was paid for by Crosby, which is the least anyone could expect a studio to do for its chief breadwinner. But unlike other studios, Crosby's outfit also foots the bill for the Continental, and the deal is quite a thing to behold. It works like this: Crosby leases the $12,000 beauty from a car rental agency and pays the rental; Vince, in turn, pays a token portion of that rental—precisely one dollar per year! Moreover, according to the arrangement, Crosby will replace the Continental with the latest model every year *Ben Casey* is on television.

The dressing room, the car, and Benny were so-called "fringe benefits" which Crosby yielded to Vince after the *Ben Casey* show sent him streaking across the Hollywood sky like a comet.

But these early kindnesses from the Crosby crowd didn't seem to instill any great qualities of humbleness in Vince. He began to demonstrate an appreciable temperament from the first time he realized that he had achieved star status, which was after the first show.

A reporter on the Coast dropped in one day to see how things were going on the set. As he entered, he heard the frightful slam of a door, then the breaking of glass. He caught a glimpse of a hulking giant striding purposefully in a prize huff, across the set toward Moser's office. The reporter recognized Vince Edwards and wondered what was bothering him.

"Oh, he just blew his stack," said one of the secondary actors playing an orderly. "They wanted him to pose for pictures on Sunday, but Vince won't go for that. It's his day off and he feels it should be his own. Everything will be straightened out. Marlon Brando does this all the time."

In something like fifteen minutes, Vince stormed out of Moser's office. One of the cameramen spotted Vince and hurried into position to shoot.

"That's good, he's still ripping," the lensman grunted. "This scene won't need any retakes."

It didn't. The script called for Vince to dress down one of the interns who had violated a hospital rule. The scene was perfect—Vince's anger oozed in every frame of the film.

But not every take comes off as well. Sometimes, in a long scene with difficult medical dialogue, they have to shoot it a dozen times before the director will call, "Okay, let's not press our luck. Print that one!" Generally, it's Vince's fault. Sometimes, it's Sam Jaffe's or Bettye Ackerman's or one of the other performer's blooper. But most often it's Vince's.

Toward the end of *Ben Casey's* first season, Vince Edwards had come to be regarded with a certain amount of disdain by the people connected with the show. Vince had contributed to this sentiment with some monumental incidents which, summed up, fall into a category known as "The Blowup."

Very often, in the middle of a scene, Vince rushes off the set in full fury and charges into the producer's office to complain bitterly about one thing or another that displeases him. Cast and crew are left in confusion and in costly idleness sometimes for as long as two hours—until Moser calms the "doctor" down.

The trouble with Vince, suggests John Edwards, a writer for London's famed *Sunday Pictorial*, is that he "hasn't enough medical savvy to worry about his own—or anyone else's—blood pressure."

The temper tantrum is expected of a star, and Vince gets away with it because he is the star of *Ben Casey*.

Once when a girlfriend wasn't allowed to drive into the studio grounds, Vince blew his top and kept the cast and crew waiting an hour until studio executives had assured him the incident would never be repeated.

The girlfriend, incidentally, was Sherry Nelson whom Vince had met shortly after his return from Japan. Sherry, a pretty, blue-eyed blonde, became Vince's favorite romantic interest. We'll come back to Sherry and the full story of the romance in another chapter.

Edwards, of course, wasn't all temperament. There was a great deal of talent there, too, for he couldn't have achieved overnight acclaim if he lacked the skills of his profession.

One of his directors agrees that Vince has an aptitude for acting, but takes exception to the widespread belief that his talents are manifold.

"Vince is limited," the director says. "Right now he plays only anger very well. That's because he is playing himself. But he's not too good in love scenes or in sequences that require comedy or humor. But I will say this about him—he's learning."

No one was more startled—and chagrined—than Vince Edwards when he failed to win the coveted Emmy for best leading actor in a 1961-'62 TV season series, or that the series itself didn't garner the best drama award. Both Vince and the show had been nominated for the honor, but neither made it.

Vince wanted to win an Emmy for himself first, and the show secondly. But either way would have made him happy—and helped Abby Greshler's plans for Vince enormously. But failure to win did not change Vince's opinion which is, that without him there wouldn't be a *Ben Casey* or, at the least, the show would not have attained its preeminence in the ratings.

Greshler felt that way, too, and the fact that neither Vince nor the show received an Emmy did not deter him from his duties as a faithful agent.

Perhaps overcome somewhat by Vince's heady post position, Greshler put the bite on Bing Crosby Productions at the end of the first season—for a raise from $1,750 a week to $7,500 a week, plus a 25 percent piece of the action and other fringe benefits over and above the $12,000 Lincoln Continental and Vince's "gofor" boy, Benny.

One of the additional fringe benefits demanded encompassed a $100,000 development fund from both the ABC network and Crosby Productions, which has sole ownership of the show. Greshler explained that the money would provide the wherewithal for the development of TV pilots for Vince's own shows of the future.

By now Vince had begun to look ahead seriously to the day when he could write, produce, direct, and act in his own video productions. In his idle days of the dozen years he had spent in Hollywood, and with the knowledge he had acquired about English during his college days, Vince wrote a number of plays—which he kept under lock and key in a trunk back in his apartment. Vince hoped to be able to put one or more of these scripts to use, once he established a reputation for himself.

However, Vince may have to postpone that day. Sad to relate, neither ABC nor Bing Crosby Productions went for the $100,000 development fund. Nor, for that matter did Crosby accede to the demands for the huge salary increase and a piece of the show.

Actually, when the terms were proposed by Greshler, the vice president in charge was so stunned by them that he kicked the matter upstairs to the boss, Crosby himself. The Groaner, no dope when it comes to business, allowed as to how he always likes to see a young fellow get ahead—but he has an aversion to fellow actors who want to cut into his profits.

As Bing saw it, Vince was trying to put the company into a spot where it wouldn't have enough in its sinking fund for the replacement of sutures, stethoscopes, and sterile gauze.

No, very definitely, no!" Bing ruled. "Give the boy a but don't give him the company."

Vince growled as he never growled before—but then the raise of $650, which brought his salary up to $2,400 a week.

Commenting on these developments, Crosby executive Carroll Nye said, "Vince can't feel too badly. He loves all the attention being heaped on him, and he doesn't dislike the fringe benefits which have been thrown his way. In fact, he delights in it. In spite of everything, though, he hasn't gotten the 'big head.' But of course he blows his cork about once a day. I guess he figures every big star is entitled to some temperament.

"It may look like he has all his problems licked, but really he hasn't. The boy is still paying off all those old debts. And only recently was he able to replenish his wardrobe, which had consisted of two suits and an old moth-eaten checkered overcoat when he first started to work as Ben Casey.

"Even though Vince didn't get his huge demands, we think he's getting quite a bit."

A sage of the Sunset Strip remarked that the Crosby turndown was the best thing that happened to Vince.

"Suppose," said the wise man, "Vince had gotten all his demands. Just imagine, he might have been so happy at getting all that money in his pay envelope each week he might have lost that look of disgust. He might even have smiled.

"Then where would he be?"

The impact Vince Edwards made on television screens in the short space of a single season was an entertainment world miracle that was reflected in the groundswell of acclaim and recognition which swept his way in 1962.

Not since 1931 when Clark Gable slapped Norma Shearer and bared his manly chest on screen had an actor caused such a whirlwind of reaction from idol-hungry fans.

The adoration for Edwards was almost universal. His earthy, direct approach to acting gave him a grip on millions of palpitating American female hearts. It was phenomenal. No TV player had ever barreled over the dames so effectively, so devastatingly.

Edwards, indeed, was to television in 1962 what Gable was to films in 1931.

Unlike Gable, however, who held the magic touch over women with his pure, unwavering masculinity, Edwards hammered his magnetism out of the elements of his television character. He was to women—and men—a knight in white surgical armor.

He was a refreshing newcomer to videoland, a welcome change from the procession of pretty-boy actors who had minced across the screen like a cute epidemic of freckles.

In his rugged, realistic portrayal of Dr. Ben Casey, Edwards was filling the abyss that traditionally stood between women and their doctors. The story of women falling in love with their physicians is as old as medicine itself, but the love is always a secret, pining feeling that remains buried.

Occasionally this sexual attachment or desire may explode resoundingly in page one scandals— *Doctor's Wife Shoots Woman Patient, Medic's Wife*

Sues Other Woman, etc. But these are rare occurrences.

Most women, being perceptive enough to sense that the attraction to their doctors is a temporary psychological fault, nurture their intimate feelings with quiet prudence.

But enter Dr. Casey on the 21-inch screen, and the ladies' secret yearnings are aroused anew at the sight of the handsome, young, virile, and masterful man in white. That gorge separating male doctor from woman patient is suddenly bridged. Even the woman's husband doesn't suspect his wife is getting a vicarious thrill from the angers, the passions, the grimaces of the impatient, brooding neurosurgeon, Casey, as he performs his psychic and physical miracles.

No wife can get in trouble with her husband if she expresses her adoration for Dr. Casey, for after all he is just another idol on the magic lamp. A flick of the dial and he's gone. Husbands feel safe with Dr. Casey in the house.

But when Edwards goes on personal appearances, it's a different story. Female hearts—from elderly and middle-aged women right down to bobbysoxers—flutter in panic. Edwards is mobbed, his clothes clawed, his ears assaulted by the squeals and sighs of his ardent admirers.

One of the most memorable in-person appearances Edwards made was in February of 1962 in Phoenix, Arizona, where 75,000 ebullient fans turned out. The occasion was the dedication of a new housing development. If one were to analyze it, the invitation to Vince Edwards to take part in this ceremony is one of society's great contradictions.

If it had been a hospital, it might have made sense!

Nevertheless, it happened.

Edwards was mobbed by the crowds who were blithering, if not idiotic, in their efforts to touch him and talk to him.

"Dr. Casey!" the women screamed hysterically, trying to approach him with their medical problems.

One middle-aged housewife broke through the mob like a Notre Dame tackle and bodily threw herself upon Edwards.

"Dr. Casey, Dr. Casey," she shouted breathlessly. "I've been trying to become pregnant for fifteen years. I never could—until I watched you on television. In three weeks, I became pregnant!

"Doctor—I have you to thank . . . only you!"

Edwards maneuvered his busy brows into a frown. His hazel eyes settled gently on the excited woman. Then, with a charming scowl, "That's very nice," he mumbled. "I'm so happy for you. But let me assure you, madam. I had nothing to do with it."

It may be a fact of life that a woman will fall in love with her doctor if he is young, virile, and handsome. But there have been plenty of young, virile, and handsome men on television and movie screens who have flopped in doctors' roles.

Vince Edwards hit it big.

Why?

In Edwards, as in few other entertainers and actors in this day and age, there is a magical "star" quality—a certain magnetism and vibrancy that captivates the beholder.

Perhaps one of the best qualified persons to analyze Edwards' grip on television audiences is the creator of the *Ben Casey* show, James Moser. Although he has all the right in the world to claim his own talents and sweat have brought the show to the forefront of television entertainment, Moser is honest enough to admit a simple truth: that Vince Edwards might have something to do with it.

"I think," Moser says, "that Edwards himself is putting *Ben Casey* over. Vince is thoroughly masculine and comes along as a provoking change from the dozens of pretty-boy actors who dominate television. But I'm certain it goes beyond that. Women look at that cave-man exterior and say to themselves, 'Beneath that hunk of rock there beats the heart of a poet.'

"It's a variation on the same theme that made big stars out of Humphrey Bogart and Clark Gable."

This writer agrees wholeheartedly with Moser. As the author of Clark Gable, the first published biography on the late actor's life, I had to delve deep into his background, as I did into Vince Edwards'. I find many similarities in their early environments, the struggling years both had spent grinding, battling, clawing their way to the top.

Not long ago, the distinguished writer, Bill Davidson, wrote a full-length article on Edwards in the *Saturday Evening Post*, entitled "TV's Surly Medico." In the story, Davidson described the similarities between Edwards and Gable as "startling." Here is how he put them:

"Both were big, rugged, unroutinely handsome, late-blooming, childlike in their pursuits of pleasure and deplorably unskilled actors when their careers finally got started. Edwards is even more impressive in bulk than Gable was. He is six feet two inches tall, weighs 210 pounds and has the general physique of a weight lifter, which he is (can 'clean and jerk' 300 pounds of barbells from the floor and lift them over his head). Just as Gable's unlovely ears gave distinction to his face, Edwards has a magnificently broken nose which prevents him, as he says, 'from looking like just another Bob Wagner.' "

The similarities, indeed, are striking.

Like Gable, Edwards had a rather untamed, undisciplined and unproductive youth. Gable quit high school, left home, worked in a rubber factory, migrated to Oklahoma to labor in the oil fields, joined a traveling carnival until it went bust, rode the rails penniless to the West, toiled further as a truck driver, lumberjack, and telephone repairman, and then finally broke into acting. But it took many more years of gritty, unrewarding effort on the legitimate stage before he cracked the imposing gates of Hollywood and ascended the golden throne of stardom.

He was thirty years old before America first awakened to his presence on the screen—after he slapped Norma Shearer in *A Free Soul.*

When the fans of 1931 viewed the sockeroo that rocked Miss Shearer almost off her feet, Gable had it made. Audiences were thrilled—men and women alike. Gable became an "overnight" success in films which led to his magnificent three-decade reign as undisputed King of the Movies.

Edwards, as we've already recounted, had his share of occupations that ran the gamut of swimmer, motorcycle racer, ditch digger, cageboy for a lion tamer, and fledgling actor playing in obscure movies predominantly as a villain.

He was thirty-three before he finally hit the big time with the *Ben Casey* show and, his impact was almost as crushing and devastating upon female hearts as Gable's. More importantly, Vince was as much a hero to the men as Gable, thanks to those thoroughly masculine animal qualities that distinguished him from the "sissy" actors.

The adulation which has crested around Edwards is a phenomenon of show business that may never cease to amaze him. Vince is at a loss to explain why success cascaded onto him so suddenly, but he is not impressed with the argument that it is so because he is the trailblazer of video's most successful medic drama series.

His instant success as Dr. Ben Casey has not greatly changed the attitude of annoyance he acquired long ago over Hollywood's failure to propel him into early stardom.

"Big deal," he growls repeatedly whenever he's complimented. "I'm a twelve-year overnight success. Nuts!"

Vince, is miffed at Hollywood for overlooking him for so long. The people at Bing Crosby Productions and ABC agree almost unanimously that he's the original angry man.

"When he snorts and snarls and gets mean in his character as Dr. Casey," a director of the show confided, "Vince isn't kidding. He's really mad."

It makes no difference to Vince that he's a dedicated servant of humanity, performing psychic and physical marvels in the make-believe of videoland. He'd just as soon play Chicago mobster Frank Nitti in *The Untouchables*.

"What's the difference what I play?" Edwards asks. "So long as they pay me, it's all the same whether I'm a mobster or a dedicated doctor. I wear a white jacket instead of a black shirt and white tie. Instead of a switch-blade knife, I wield a scalpel. Instead of a gun, I carry a stethoscope. Big deal—after a dozen years of my life."

But Eliot Ness, who has been tracking down mobster Nitti week after week in the Walter Winchell hour-long gangland extravaganza, never hit it quite as big as Ben Casey. And therein lies a profound clue—the age-old love of a woman for her doctor.

Despite his unique and questionable philosophy on the portent of his success, Edwards even now cannot help but stand in awe at the overwhelming reception and recognition he has received.

At the time of his personal appearance stint in Phoenix, Edwards was stunned at the turnout of 75,000 fans.

"The Mayor told me," Vince recalled, "that he wished the people would turn out like that for an election."

Although he appreciated the crowd's response, Vince couldn't shake the bitterness he feels inside.

"Before Ben Casey went on the air," he said tartly, "I could have pushed a peanut down the main street of Phoenix and the only one who would have cared would have been the cop who arrested me.

"Everybody says I have it made. But I still haven't felt the impact. It happened too quickly—after nearly twelve years. Maybe it's because I don't have time to think about it too much. Ben Casey keeps me hopping. I've got seventy pages of script to memorize every week. I've got to get up at 6 A.M. every day. I'm at the studio until it gets dark. After that I've barely got time to take a girl out for dinner. By ten o'clock at night I'm beat and the only thing on my mind then is sleep."

If he is short on time in checking up on how greatly success has come his way, there are many who have found intervals to measure Vince's progress. His mother, Julie Zoine, and the other members of Vince's family have spent endless hours accumulating scrap books of their favorite star's press clippings. The volumes are building up like a dam during a flood. Hardly a day goes by that some columnist doesn't mention Vince Edwards. Hardly a month passes that one, two, or more movie and/or television fan magazines fail to do a feature on videoland's most popular actor.

Even the Sunday rotogravure sections have begun to feature Vince's busy-browed, Valentino-like mug on their covers. When the *New York News* published a cover photo of Vince in their Sunday Coloroto Magazine, his photogenic image made a smashing impact upon his women idolaters. The picture, taken by Harry. Warnecke and Gus Schoenbaechler, showed Vince in an open-collar white sport shirt and red wool button-down-the-front sweater. His hazel eyes gazed languidly into the lens. His lips were edged in a faint smile. His black hair reflected the blazing light of the photographers' studio which gave it a semi-oily look, with glistening strands of white coursing through it. These were not streaks of gray. but simply light waves bouncing off the lubricous hairs. It gave Vince just the right touch of maturity.

The picture, circulating as it did to the *News'* 3,125,000 loyal Sunday readers, hit like a bombshell. The concussion shook the women hardest. They reacted like true fans, inundating the *News* with thousands of letters that expressed their delight over the newspaper's good sense in publishing Vince's photo on its rotogravure cover.

Ben Casey may be violent at times, angry at other times, surly in the remaining time. Which doesn't leave time for smiles.

Yet Vince Edwards apparently was just what the doctor ordered for TV's ailing ratings. Playing the title role in *Ben Casey*, 1962's most popular show, Vince has found his way on 32,000,000 home television sets every Monday night via ABC-TV.

The doctor image which Vince so effectively put across the airwaves in his first season has entitled him to enjoy an unprecedented popularity that amazes even the most astute students of the phenomenon called stardom.

Clark Gable never had it so good—not even after nearly a dozen years in show business.

11
THE WOMAN IN VINCE'S LIFE

OVERHEAD, a brilliant spring sun stared down on the Santa Anita racetrack and upon the galaxy of fantastic horseflesh that had been rounded up for the $100,000 Futurity. It was still an hour before post time but the crowd was already on hand, poring over the forms and tout sheets in preparation for the big race.

Down in the paddock among the coterie of special guests invited by the owners to look over the entries, were two extraordinarily good-looking blondes, standing immersed in sunlight and oblivious to admiring glances of the two handsome men next to them.

Then suddenly the girls turned and spotted the men. One was Benny Goldberg, the former middleweight boxer from Brooklyn. The other was Vince Edwards.

This was B.C.—*Before Casey*. It was spring, 1960, and the world had not yet been introduced to the angry, surly Dr. Ben Casey. But one of the girls recognized the face. She had seen it in gangster films. She couldn't remember the name. But she knew the possessor of that face was an actor.

"An actor, I know he's an actor," she whispered to her blonde companion.

Then the companion, Sherry Nelson, a lovely former fashion model of twenty-two, turned and looked at the brooding actor. He smiled, his dark eyes fixed steadily upon her. He came over with Benny, who was Vince's friend, and spoke.

"How do you do. I'm Vince Edwards. This is Benny Goldberg."

Sherry didn't seem to pay much attention to the tall, dark, muscular man, but her best friend, Marty Dickerson, flipped.

Polite conversation went back and forth among them. Sherry didn't seem surprised when Vince asked for her phone number. Lots of handsome young men asked for her phone number.

But Marty Dickerson was ecstatic. She couldn't take her eyes off rugged Vince, who was so much more alive, so vibrant, so different in person than the man she'd remembered on the screen. And so different than most young men she knew. This was, definitely, a "somebody."

Yet, Sherry felt nothing on that first, casual meeting, and was stunned to discover the effect Vince had had on her friend.

Because, when Vince sauntered away in his un-assuming manner, Marty breathed an exaggerated sigh, stared after him, and blurted, "I've just met the man I'm going to marry!"

Sherry gasped, glanced after the retreating Vince, and said, "You're out of your mind!"

But it wasn't Marty that Vince was interested in, as it became obvious a few days later. Sherry, who hadn't paid much attention, received a phone call. It was Vince.

The rugged actor asked her for a dinner date, and even then she didn't know if she cared to. But she decided to take a second look at him. Sherry invited him to drop by the comfortable apartment she shared with her mother.

"I could still get out of the dinner date if I didn't care for his appearance on second look," Sherry explained later.

The second look was *something*. Somehow, the unassuming and not overly interesting young actor had been replaced by a brooding, sensitive giant of a man who dwarfed his surroundings. Sherry was on the phone when her mother let Vince in, and she was able to watch him enter.

"I stopped in my tracks, amazed," she recalled. "Somehow, in the vast outdoors, I had acquired no comprehension of the size of the man. He made our doorway seem totally inadequate. He dwarfed the modern furnishings of our room."

There stood a towering, six-foot-two, two-hundred-and-ten-pound hulk of a man with shoulders like a professional football halfback, radiating power, and looking like a real-life Tarzan than any of the sad substitutes yearned for such a role. A great head of long, flowing hair crowned him majestically, giving him the appearance of a huge St. Bernard.

He saw her looking at the lionlike mane and moved his hand to his head self-consciously. "I'm not like this all the time," Vince grinned. "I just finished a part in *The Deputy*—as a frontier doctor—and you know how those guys looked."

"We had a good laugh together," Sherry said.

Actually Sherry was able to look beyond the hulking appearance and detect something else. It was there in the alert eyes, the quick fluid conversation. It spoke of intelligence, a nimble mind.

"To tell you the truth," Sherry recalls, "if I hadn't known him, I would have judged him to be a young attorney of early and exceptional success. Or possibly a corporation officer. Perhaps a Madison Avenue type in his well-tailored dark blue suit, his white shirt, and his conservative tie. Or even a quiet, dedicated young neurosurgeon. But certainly not an actor."

Sherry and Vince sat about chatting pleasantly when Sherry's mother entered the room. If she had made any quick appraisal of Vince she didn't show it, but instead joined in conversation and stayed about a half hour. All the while Sherry kept waiting

194

for a signal from her mother. It was part of a long-standing routine. Sherry, of course, was not a child, and was fully capable of mature, common-sense decisions herself. But because of deeply ingrained respect for her mother's wishes, and because experience had taught her that sometimes, after all, mother really does know best, she refused to date anyone who failed to pass muster with Mom.

"It didn't take long," Sherry says. "Mother stayed and talked and then got up and said she had a bridge date with friends. As she talked, she gave me the nod. It was okay to have dinner with Vince."

And that was the beginning of what has become one of the most durable boy-girl romances Hollywood has ever seen. But it's not a man-wife relationship. Not yet. Maybe not ever. And yet Sherry Nelson is the one girl Vince Edwards, the rocketing star, has persistently dated, the one person he feels closer to than anyone else on earth.

They are reluctant to talk about it, but it's manifestly clear they love each other. Certainly they don't deny the almost daily rumors that have them half-way down to the altar already. And the chances are good that by the time this reaches print, their wedding will be yesterday's story.

Well, then, what sort of romance did they have after they met, to strengthen the powerful bond between them which exists today? Let Sherry herself describe it.

"That first evening set the pattern. We went to the Villa Capri where Vince ordered the most terrific Italian dinner I ever tasted. We lingered over the wine, and then went to The Little Club to hear a singer I'd heard a lot about. We had a wonderful time and a lot of laughs, and then we went home, sort of early, I guess you'd say.

"And it's been more or less like that ever since. We get together when Vince is able to spare the time. He usually asks me if I have a preference about where to go, but usually I leave it to him. He really knows his way around town."

As their friendship grew, so did their knowledge of one another, each becoming aware of the other's habits, tastes, likes and dislikes.

"I soon found that Vince is a gourmet," Sherry recalled, camouflaging any surprise she may have felt in her discovery. "He knows Cantonese cookery, Japanese foods, Hawaiian foods, French cuisine, and, naturally, the best of Italian dishes. He likes to take a group out to dinner and order the menu from hors d'ouvres to dessert. It's a treat, believe me. I had spent my life as a roast-beef-and-baked-potato addict, so an entire gastronomic world opened up to my astonished palate."

Vince's enthusiasm about food goes more for his guests than for himself. He is still an "organic foods man," as he says, and will not indulge himself in the luxuriant foods served at the restaurants and night clubs he visits with friends. Occasionally he'll break "training," but only occasionally.

His interest in food is actually a corollary to his interest in physical fitness that goes back to his days as a youth and as a swimmer at Ohio State and the University of Hawaii.

Hawaii has always held a fascination for Vince, and he shares a particular daydream he has with Sherry.

"I love to hear him talk about the islands," she says. "In that daydream, he plans a glamor-filled holiday. In this fantasy, he charters a jet and flies a group of friends to Honolulu where everyone stays at the Royal Hawaiian Hotel, but seldom uses the rooms except for a change of clothing. For a week, this house party on wings swims, goes surfing, joins in out-rigger canoe races, attends luaus, goes to Japanese tea houses, dances in the moonlight . . . 'I'll be able to do it someday,' Vince says, coming to earth with a grin, 'just you wait and see.'

"I believe him."

The dream is reflective of another tangent to Vince Edwards' personality. It's his extraordinary generosity.

"Generous and thoughtful," says Sherry, "particularly in his gift-giving." She remembers their second date.

"He brought me a three-yard length of cashmere that he obtained in Hong Kong. He said, 'When I bought it, I planned to have a sports jacket tailored, but I knew after our Sunday night date that I wanted to give it to you. You're a natural for that shade.' It was a beautiful gray with the shadow over-plaid, and if you don't mind a little immodesty, it did look great on me.

For Christmas, 1960, Vince gave Sherry a terrific pullover sweater.

"Ordinarily," Sherry said, "I wear conservative colors. But Vince spotted this number in a window. It was black with narrow stripes of turquoise, lavender, and gold. He told me, 'You wear so much black it seems to me this would look wonderful with all your sports things.' And again, to be frank, it did. Vince certainly does have taste."

On Christmas Day, 1961, Sherry found a note from Vince in the Christmas card he sent. He had ordered an Aquascutum raincoat from London for Sherry.

"Naturally I flipped," Sherry smiled. "The rain-coat *finally* arrived on February 5, and so help me, on February 7 California got the first of a five-day cloudburst. Vince still believes it was all my fault for wishing for rain so hard."

With one gift, Vince displayed his puckish sense of humor.

"When I had all four of my wisdom teeth extracted at once," Sherry remembers, "Vince showed up at the house bearing very understanding words of sympathy. I thought it was so sweet of him.

"Then he gave me a three-pound box of chocolates!"

Like all sensible girls, Sherry Nelson knows that to keep a man's interest, she must please him, and keep pleasing him, even if it means accommodating herself to a few new and untried ideas about dress, hairdos, and the like. Sherry had one such experience.

"Vince has definite ideas about the appearance of the girl he's dating," she says. "I remember that after I had five or six dates with Vince, I rushed to a beauty shop and had myself done over . . . as I imagine many girls in the same spot do. I had my simple upswept ponytail turned into a swirling beehive, and I'd bought a new beige lace and brown satin dress that I thought represented the ultimate in chic. I could scarcely wait for Vince to arrive that evening.

"He looked me over carefully and complimented me on my hair and my gown. But something was wrong. I could sense it. He kept strolling around, delaying our departure for some friends' house where we'd been invited for dinner.

"Then it finally burst out of him. 'Would you mind,' he said, looking like Dr. Casey prescribing a serious operation, 'would you mind recombing your hair into the usual ponytail? And would you be annoyed if I asked you to wear that wonderful black dress?'

"That 'wonderful black dress'—and I've worn it many times since—is chiffon over satin. It has a rather high boat neck, long transparent sleeves and a snug bodice and a very full skirt.

"Naturally I redid my hair and changed into the chiffon. What's the fun of a date if you feel your escort is vaguely uncomfortable because of your appearance?

"Since I'm blonde, I've always worn a great deal of pink, but Vince doesn't care for the color on me. He prefers that I wear only powder blue, beige, or black. I must say his taste is good, because I've had more compliments on my appearance and wardrobe during the time I've been going with Vince than I've ever had before.

"I realize that some girls would resist Vince's firm ideas, but I believe a girl should dress to please the man she's dating. It would be silly to permit a trivial thing like a choice of wardrobe to create a disturbance between two people."

Not, Sherry feels, that Vince would get really riled up about it.

"He has a very easy-going, undemanding nature," she says. "But he can get mad, believe me. I've seen it.

"He can get wrought up about injustice, general stupidity, or wild selfishness in traffic as the next man. On occasion he blows up like a volcano. But when it's over— it's over. And twenty minutes later it would be hard for him to remember why he had been so exasperated. He is incapable of holding a grudge or planning revenge."

There is yet another aspect of the multi-prismed Vince Edwards that endears him to Sherry: his modesty.

"It's really one of his most attractive traits," she says. "He still can't believe that he's been accepted as the dedicated, dynamic, toughly tender Dr. Ben Casey. He is sharply critical of the work of Vince Edwards, actor, and constantly strives for a more sensitive, more perceptive, more authentic portrayal of the talented neurosurgeon.

"Vince is unabashedly pleased when doctors, seeing him in a restaurant or other public place, go out of their way to tell him that he is doing a fine job for the medical profession and that they are grateful to the producers, directors, writers, and actors responsible for the series.

"And when girls approach him with those big, open, worshipful eyes and long-drawn sighs, he accepts their admiration with understanding and humility. He tells me, 'Their admiration isn't intended for me, but for Dr. Ben Casey. I never forget that for a moment.'

"Nor is Vince Edwards one to flaunt his new-found wealth. For a long time he'd been driving an old coffee pot of a car. Then when the studio gave him the Lincoln Continental, he was happy. But when we attended a premiere a few weeks after he had gotten the car, he parked it several blocks away from the theater in preference to driving it grandly up to the entrance. We walked to the red carpet as we had always done during the days when Vince was driving his Old Broken Bucket."

All of which, as Sherry explains, is why she thinks Vince Edwards is "one of the nicest human beings I have ever met; he's a pleasant, thoughtful companion, a loyal friend, and a highly talented workman in a difficult and demanding field."

Sherry Nelson had made Vince Edwards forget other girls. He stopped dating and gave all his attention to Sherry. Forgotten were Liz Scott, Shelley Winters, Cleo Moore, and Sandra Giles.

And Michiko.

Michiko?

Well, almost but not completely. For Michiko came back briefly into Vince Edwards' life. Very briefly.

It happened recently. Vince was leaving the set of *Ben Casey* when one of the directors called him over.

"Vince, here's someone I'd like you to meet."

Vince stared at the girl before him. She held his glance. They said nothing.

"This is Michiko," the director said cheerily. "She's a friend of mine. Her father's here on business. Michiko, meet Vince Ed . . . Vince! What's wrong?"

Then he turned toward Michiko. She was wiping a tear from her eye.

"I must have something in my eye. Would you take it out . . . Vince?" she asked, forcing a smile at the man who once had meant more than life itself to her.

They explained their "friendship" to the director, and he left them alone. There was an awkward silence. They filled it as best they could. How was the weather? Fine. How is Tokyo? Same as always. Has that little supper club changed? Do you like your work, Vince? How is your father? And on. And on. Trivia. Inanities. What do you say to a person when you don't dare mention the only thing either one is really thinking about?

And so they parted. Today, Michiko is married. Only Vince and Michiko, in the deepest corners of their hearts, know how strong their feeling is for one another, whether some fragment of their long-ago love still abides there or whether the ever-moving tides of life have washed away the past forever.

Anyway, it seems that the swift currents of romance have brought Vince to the shores of a new era with Sherry. Yet for all her obvious and self-proclaimed admiration and fondness for Vince (and what those who know them describe as love), Sherry is both self-conscious about her relationship with the handsome actor and a bit hesitant to call it anything but "friendship."

"Maybe this will explain it," she says. "I was at a nightclub recently with Vince. As I was freshening my lipstick in the powder room, a wonderfully pretty girl came up to me and said with sighs and rolling eyes, 'Man, how I dig those crazy diseases since I've been watching Vince Edwards in *Ben Casey*. I'd as soon spend the rest of my life in a hospital just to be near him. I think you're the luckiest girl in the world to be his one and only.'

"Frankly, her words upset me. Look. I'm a widow. My husband and I—both just eighteen— were married two weeks after we were graduated from Burbank High School in 1955. Six months later he was killed in an accident. I live comfortably with my mother and my kooky French poodle 'Corky.'

204

"As for Vince, he scarcely has time to eat three meals a day, to say nothing of carrying on a heavy courtship—or trying to maintain a marriage. What he needs at this particular point in his professional life is a girl chum who has no commitments, makes no demands, loves life and laughter, and finds happiness in each day for that day's sake. That's where I fit into the picture. We have a happy-hearted, undemanding mutually understanding status with each other. I'm a friend—and I hope a loyal and helpful one."

All of which, for Sherry, is the proper thing to say. She knows Vince Edwards has come a long way and that the road ahead is, very likely, limitless for him. All he needs is time, time to find his own way in life and in love. And he can't be pushed in either.

At least no one can push Vince Edwards.

In early June, 1962, the ABC offices in New York City were aflutter with a rumor that Vince Edwards was coming home for a visit with his mother. The flying report spread like pollen during hayfever season and soon everyone was wheezing: Vince is coming. Columnists in the metropolitan area printed it.

I called Vince's mother at her apartment in Brooklyn to learn if she was aware of her son's impending return.

"Yes," she replied, "I know it."

Her voice drifted. I asked what was wrong.

"He was coming home, and the whole family was getting ready for him. But then there was a sudden change in plans. He had to go to Indianapolis—to do publicity for the Memorial Day 500-mile race. He was forced to cancel his plans . . ."

I asked if this meant that Vince would not come home to visit. It had been twelve long years since he left for Hollywood and, except for that brief, unhappy trip East to attend his father's funeral, Vince had not returned home since.

"No, no," Mama Julie Zoine cried with alarm. She didn't want *me* to misunderstand, too. There had been many rumors—rumors in the columns that Vince didn't want to come home again; that since he hit the big-time he had forgotten his family and friends back in Brooklyn; that perhaps, like the Dodgers, he had forsaken Brooklyn for good. Mrs. Zoine was apprehensive.

"Please," she beseeched, "Vince was *forced* to change his plans. He called up last night and begged me to understand. But he didn't have to do that— I always understand when Vinnie talks to me. I know how difficult his life is and how complicated it's made with his hectic work schedule. He told me to wait . . ."

There was no resentment in Mama Julie's voice. There was a hint of disappointment but, after all, she was his mother; whatever her Vinnie was doing was all right with her.

"He'll be here as soon as he can get clear from his obligations," she said with a confidence that only a mother can express in her son.

Mama Julie had waited a long time for the visit. A short delay, as Vinnie had promised, was not going to disappoint her. Mrs. Zoine was as happy and proud as a mother can be of a son who stood at the pinnacle of success, and for her there was more happiness and pride because her son's triumphs on television as Ben Casey had brought her into the spotlight as a celebrity, as it did other members of Vince's family, too.

Julie herself, however, was exposed to the adulation of the masses in far greater dosages than the others in the family, for she was in daily touch with one of the age groups which has literally flipped its wig over Vince Edwards—teenagers. Julie today is still the hard-working, self-supporting mother she was back a dozen years or more ago when she went to the Board of Education for a job to help pay for Vinnie's way through drama school. She still works in the cafeteria in Brooklyn's Eli Whitney Vocational High School.

"It's a wonderful job," Mama Julie told me. "I love it and I love to serve food to the children . . ."

Her work naturally brings her in direct contact with the kids, and that makes Mama Julie a celebrity since she is the mother of TV's most famous physician. Mrs. Zoine laughed as she related how it is.

"The new kids who come to the school give me the biggest kick," she said. "They come over to me and say, 'Are you really Ben Casey's mother?' They seem to think that the mother of a big star like Vince Edwards should not work—especially at such a routine thing like a countergirl's job. But I tell them before they have a chance to say it. I tell them, 'I know you'll ask me what I'm doing here. My answer is that I love you all . . .' "

The kids who meet Julie Zoine for the first time are very surprised and don't seem able to believe it, even after the veteran students have confirmed what she already said about being Vince's mother.

"The children are all well-behaved. Once they get to know me, all they want to do is talk about Vinnie. They keep asking me the same question you ask—when will he come home? And they also want to know if they might have a chance to see him. I tell them to be patient."

Vince's twin brother, Bob Zoine, has also been dipped in some of the glare from the intense light of publicity that has saturated his famous twin. Bob today drives a bus for the New York City Transit Authority; he has been married nearly thirteen years and lives with his wife, Ginger, and their two daughters, Gina, who is going on five, and Karen, going on two, in a lovely ranch house in Westbury, Long Island.

In fact, the house is just four blocks down the street from mine. Bob's my neighbor. His kids and my kids go, or will go eventually, to the same school. His wife and my wife shop in the same stores, buy the same bargains. Bob and I buy grass seed and fertilizer form the same nursery, nails from the same hardware store, lumber from the same lumberyard. He builds concrete patios and lays bricks around his house. Thank God I don't anymore. I've finished mine. Bob wishes he were through, too.

I sympathize with him for being Vince Edwards' twin, which Bob often finds can be harrowing and annoying. But sometimes it's good for laughs. Bob is a down-to-earth soul. He has no airs. There's no prima donna in him.

"All I want," Bob says, "is to be left alone. I love my job as a bus driver. I make a good living and I make enough to provide my family with the necessities and a few luxuries of life. What else does a guy need?"

Bob's bus route covers three of the city's five boroughs—Brooklyn, Bronx, and Queens. Twice a week he tools a lumbering sixty-seat Transit Authority bus over the Flatbush Avenue line in

Brooklyn. The other three days he's a jockey on the route between West Farms Square in the Bronx to Jamaica, Queens.

Bob likes to avoid people who want to meet him because he's Vince Edwards' twin brother. But when he's behind the wheel of the bus, he can't very well escape that fate. Most of the time he finds it annoying when someone gets on the bus and says, "Oh, you're Ben Casey's twin!"

Occasionally, however, he gets a kick out of it. For example, one day not long ago he was ready to start his Bronx-Queens run. Just as he was about to close the door, a dozen kids in Boy Scout uniforms charged down the street waving frantically to the driver. Bob held the door open. The kids piled into the bus, breathless.

"Hooray!" screamed the first one aboard. "We've found him! It's Ben Casey's twin brother!"

The youngsters screamed ecstatically. They dropped their fares into the coin box and swarmed around Bob as he started on the run.

"You know," said one of the kids to Bob, who was amused by the enthusiasm, "we've been riding the buses for days looking for you. And now we've found you!"

Then they plied Bob with questions about Vince. Bob was hard-pressed all the way to the Ja-maica terminal answering the kids' queries—while managing the behemoth bus safely to its destination.

Another time, the Transit Authority held a ceremony to dedicate a new 1962 bus that was being introduced into service. They invited the press to cover the event.

And whom did the TA call to sit behind the wheel?

Yup—Bob Zoine!

A few days after my inquiry to Mama Julie about Vince's homecoming, I called again. This time there was a lilt in her voice as she greeted me.

"He's here!" she exclaimed.

Mrs. Zoine told me that Vinnie had arrived in the city that morning and had taken a suite in the Hampshire House.

"We're going to get together tomorrow at Bob's house in Westbury," she said. "The whole family will be there."

It was quite a shindig. Everyone turned out— Mama Julie, big brother, Joe, sister, Nancy, all the kids.

And Sherry Nelson was there also, along with Nick Dennis and Benny Goldberg. Nick and Benny are so close to Vince that he wouldn't dream of not bringing them along to meet the family.

It was to have been a simple family get-together, but it nearly turned into a route—or riot.

Just visualize the scene. Vince drove up in his big studio-rented limousine and parked in front of Bob's modest but sprawling ranch house. Somehow, the kids in the block got wind that Ben Casey was visiting his twin brother.

Panic!

Kids from blocks away swanned around the house, trampling the lawn, climbing the trees, and overrunning the neighbors' properties. It was a madhouse of screaming, squealing youngsters. There must have been a hundred of them.

There was nothing Bob or Benny or Nick or Joe could do to clear the kids away. Even a plea from Vince failed—it only drove the youngsters into pandemonium.

Finally, the Nassau County Police were called. Three radio cars came, six patrolmen. They had their hands full but they managed to dispel the mob.

When Vince arrived, his mother was inside the house. He went to the door, opened it, and walked in.

"Hi, Mom," he said with a big smile, putting out his arms.

Mama Julie looked at Vince for a moment with trembling lips. Then she rushed into his arms as Vince tightened them into a bear hug and kissed her. Mam Julie kissed her son repeatedly as she wept for joy; Vince had tears in his eyes, too.

"It's the happiest moment of my life," she told her famous son. "You've come home . . ."

Vince then introduced his friends—Sherry, Benny, and Nick.

Later, much later, when Vince and his mother were alone, Mrs. Zoine wanted to know about Sherry. She had read about the pretty blue-eyed blonde in the fan magazines and the columns.

Today, Mama Julie Zoine is sixty-seven years old but she can walk the legs off a young chick—and often does on her strolls through Brooklyn. She's sixty-seven years old and so very alive. And glad to be so.

But she's also at an age that a mother likes to see a son, just about half her age now, take the big step toward marriage, a home, and children. Vince is the last of Mrs. Zoine's four surviving children who has not yet answered the tingle of wedding bells. More than anything in the world, Mama Julie wants that to happen. The sooner the better.

"So, tell me, Vinnie," she prodded her prodigal son, "are you going to marry this girl? Before you answer, let me tell you something—I like her very much."

Vinnie smiled and took his mother's hand tenderly.

"Sherry is a very fine girl," he began. "She stuck with me when I had nothing . . ."

When Vince met Sherry at Santa Anita back in 1959, he was nearly flat broke. He had just finished *Too Late Blues* and his career was still wallowing in a quagmire of uncertainty.

"I dated Sherry during the tough days and she was every bit as sweet and nice then as she is now—now that I have something. Do you think I'd let go of a girl like her?"

But Mrs. Zoine wanted to know what Vince's plans with Sherry were for the future.

"Sure I'm thinking about getting married and having kids," Vince told his mother. "What guy in his right mind doesn't? But I believe marriage is for keeps and forever. With Sherry, marriage is for keeps and forever, too.

"When I think of a wife, I think of a girl who'd be so nice to come home to. Who'd be waiting at the door for me with a big smile, ready to throw her arms around And kiss me. And make me feel that I belong there—with her.

"Marriage is a permanent contract and that's what I want it to be for me.

"Sure I want to get married—and that's why I'm going steady with Sherry. She thinks of marriage in the same ways that I do.

"Just give me a little time. You'll see . . ."

Mrs. Zoine heard what she had wanted to hear. At sixty-seven, she is animated—she's full of life, full of spirit, full of bounce and buoyancy. She bubbles with breeziness.

She had exercised a mother's prerogative and asked her famous son just exactly what Sherry Nelson meant to him. The reply was what Mama Julie wanted to hear, and it gave her life a little more meaning, a little more promise, something to look forward to.

After the visit, Vince went back to Hollywood. A month later, he flew to London to begin work on *The Victors*. He departed amid faint rumblings of discord with Sherry. It seems that some enterprising savants of the fourth estate spotted Vince out with Diane McBaine, the former Miss Rheingold queen.

"It's a lousy thing to do," Vince complained bitterly. "Now Sherry will be terribly upset while I'm gone."

But when Vince went to the airport, it was Sherry who went along to wave goodbye.

Everything in England was as Vince had expected, except for one change which occurred when producer Carl Foreman took a bus ride. He was sitting on the top of a double-decker weaving through Piccadilly Circus.

"The weather was wonderful," said Foreman. "Everything was fine. I was looking forward to the start of production. And then it happened."

He glanced down and saw a huge newspaper headline.

"Sophia Loren—Bigamy Trial!"

Foreman hopped off the bus at the next stop, rushed to his office in a cab, and phoned Sophia.

"It's true," she told Foreman. "My husband and I have been ordered to stand trial on technical charges of bigamy . . . Oh, Carl, I feel condemned."

Miss Loren and her husband, Italian producer Carlo Ponti, were married by proxy in Mexico in 1957, three years after Ponti's Mexican divorce. But in Italy divorce is illegal!

With Miss Loren tied up in an impending court case, Foreman could not risk delays that could crop up during production. The film was on a tight one-month schedule. Vince was committed to return in mid-September to Hollywood to resume work on *Ben Casey*. So Foreman was forced to take precautions.

He looked around for a replacement for Miss Loren—and found her in the sultry Italian beauty Rosanna Schiaffino.

Working with Rosanna, with George Peppard and George Hamilton and other stars, Vince was a different person than he is on the *Ben Casey* set. There were no outlandish displays of temperament, no serious interruptions in shooting because one thing or another displeased him.

Why? Why did Vince suddenly change in the company of some of the world's great stars, stars with stature and talent deemed by many as superior to his own. Was it inferiority complex or stage fright or perhaps the belief that he was now in company with actors and actresses who provided an acting yardstick to measure his dramatic ability with his intern's coat off?

Vince won't say, but it's clear enough in his explanation of why he is so difficult and temperamental on the *Ben Casey* sound stage.

"I'm playing Casey," Vince says. "So it's I who can tell if Casey's doing right. If he's not, I know it and I must correct Casey's mistakes."

In doing *The Victors*, Vince Edwards was hoping that he could bring the day closer when he can shed the Ben Casey mantle and emerge into a full-blown movie star, which is the goal he had set for himself from the very beginning. It is a goal he has never lost sight of—not even with the great success and wealth and adulation that has come to him from his television role.

"I give myself three years," he says. "That's about all of my life that I can give to *Ben Casey*. After that, I've got to look for bigger and more important roles . . ."

Vince has great plans for the future. He wants to write dramas. He wants to direct them. He wants to produce them. And act in them.

Vince Edwards with a frown and formaldehyde, has helped supplant violence and bloodshed on television and prompted a large segment of American TV watchers to regard hypochondria as the most important form of entertainment.

Perhaps three years is a long time on one series. Perhaps not. Today, hypochondria is the prime lure of television and if anyone wants proof, just look at the 1962-'63 fall-winter season of TV programs. Audiences were up to their eyeballs in stethoscopes and sutures and formaldehyde as eight new series were ground out frenziedly and sold for air time by producers anxious to cash in on the medical craze engendered by *Ben Casey*.

As this biography on Vincent Edwards goes to press, there seems to be no antitoxin in sight to cure Ben Casey-itis—a national disease which has added a new dimension to the shower of hot electrons that stream from a video camera.

12
DR. ZORBA EXAMINES DR. CASEY (SAM JAFFE ON VINCE EDWARDS)

"HE'S THE YOUNG MAN I once wanted to be."

Sam Jaffe, who was handpicked by Jim Moser for the role of Dr. David Zorba in *Ben Casey*, advanced that tribute the first week he was on the set with Vince Edwards. He was impelled to remark about the young star of the show because Jaffe saw a good deal of himself in the brooding, frowning countenance that was destined to galvanize panic among American womanhood.

There are many similarities between Jaffe and Edwards. The first to admit this is Sam's wife, Bettye Ackerman. We'll hear her views in the next chapter, but for now let's see how Vince and Sam shape up as a team—both as actors and as make-believe doctors in the biggest medical drama in television history.

When Sam Jaffe remarked how he'd like to have been the type of young man Vince is, he was speaking to Bettye. Vince wasn't within earshot. Yet, later, when Bettye went over to Vince and asked him about Sam, the answer she received sounded as though Vince had been eavesdropping.

"I like Sam," Vince said, "because I see in him the man I'd like to become . . ."

Bettye's questions were prompted by her fast-growing realization that a strong bond of friendship had developed from the outset between her husband and the dark, handsome young Dr. Casey during the long and tedious days each spent in the preparation of the series at Desilu Studios.

The fondness—call it devotion—that blossomed between Vince and Sam may be rooted in their common backgrounds. Both come from New York; Vince is from Brooklyn, Sam from Manhattan's East Side. Their families were both hard-pressed in making ends meet and both men had to struggle up the ladder to success. As youths, each had a strong desire for education. And they were to a very large extent self-made men. No one handed Vince or Sam any favors on a silver platter—they struggled and sacrificed and sweated to reach the top.

Jaffe has been a successful actor since before Vince was born, back in the faraway heydays of Al Jolson and George Jessel. In fact, Jaffe had second billing behind Jessel, the star, in the 1926 Broadway musical smash, The Jazz Singer, which Warner Brothers later made into a milestone movie—the first talkie—with Al Jolson.

From the very beginning of his career, it was apparent that Jaffe was enhancing the entertainment world's stature with his presence. He came to be regarded as one of the few brains in acting, for he had given up a career as a teacher of mathematics to go behind the footlights.

Additionally, Jaffe acquired a profound interest and high skill as a pianist, then as a language buff. Today, Sam speaks Italian, French, German, Hebrew, and Japanese; he reads calculus books for pleasure! And since he has been heavily committed to play the second most important character in B*en Casey*, he has surrounded himself with medical dictionaries and books, studying and memorizing the language of the physician. His medical vocabulary grows daily in leaps and bounds—and the proof of his extensive understanding is to be found in the invitation to address that medical convention in Chicago.

Allan Warner, the neurosurgeon retained as technical adviser on the *Ben Casey* set, often casts a wary eye on Jaffe as he pores through the medical tomes. And it causes Warner to wonder.

"They won't need me on the show in a few more months," he says. "Jaffe will know all the answers by then. Jaffe will also probably be operating at Los Angeles County General Hospital by then, and I'll be out of a job."

No one appreciates Jaffe's intense interest and thorough buildup in medical terminology as much as Ben Casey himself.

"I don't dig this neurosurgical jazz too well," says Vince. "I'm glad to have Sam nearby to straighten me out."

One of those times that Sam "straightened out" Vince came during rehearsal of a hospital sequence dealing with the Babinski test, which is a neurological diagnostic procedure.

"All right," Vince cracked, obviously jesting, "let's get ready for the bagel test."

Jaffe, not quick on the draw in sensing the intended humor, took Vince to task.

"No, no, no!" he shouted. "It's Babinski—B-A-B-I-N-S-K-I. You've got to say it properly. It's a very important medical term."

Vince smiled politely, shaking his head.

"I'm sorry, Sam, I was just kidding."

Jaffe strode up to the towering Vince, clenched a fist, and shook it in his face menacingly but good-naturedly.

"Tu sta tropo giovane per un nero ochio."

Vince looked at Jaffe in bewilderment.

"Say it in English, Doc," he said. "You know my mother never could teach me Italian."

Dr. Zorba then translated.

"You are too young for a black eye."

Although Jaffe is small in stature, he is masculine and, in many respects, a condensed physical version of the Adonis-like Vince Edwards.

Both Vince and Sam have many similar traits. They are strong-willed, serious in their work, and idealistic. Both are generous men and have a deep and abiding compassion for the underdog.

In that respect, Jaffe has been approached through the years by struggling actors for a hand in steering them to jobs, or simply for a handout. In his generous way, Sam has helped many a starving actor find work—or made substantial loans to them. Through the years, he has suffered some unfortunate experiences when it came to lending money—and he had not infrequently noticed that Vince, now that he had hit it big, was being approached by some of his pals of the old tough days.

One day, finally, Sam took Vince aside to give him some advice.

"Vince, you've got to use discretion when you hand out money," Jaffe said. "You can lose a friend very quickly when you lend him dough."

"Thanks, Sam," replied Vince. "I'll remember that."

Some days later, an old acquaintance approached Vince and put the bite on him. Jaffe's warning was still in Edwards' mind. He dug into his pocket and handed the chum a ten, the minimum Vince felt he should give.

The friend took the money but left disgustedly. He walked over to Sam and sang his song of woe anew. Sam, perhaps, had forgotten his lecture to Vince, or more likely, his generosity held too much sway over his words of wisdom. Sam gave the down-and-out actor a sizable loan.

Vince happened by just as the transaction was concluded. His eyes fired up in rage.

"So! So, Doctor," Vince snarled after the borrower left, "this you call medical ethics—you diagnose my condition, then practice the exact opposite! What kind of physician are you? Such a schnook!"

Sam Jaffe was dumbstruck. His voice paralyzed, he had nothing to say. He shrugged sheepishly, like a kid caught with his hand in the cookie jar.

Their relationship on the set has grown into a strong bond of friendship off-camera as well. After the first year's filming was completed and the shows were in the can, the cast was given a vacation before beginning work on another year's production. Vince decided to go with Sam and Bettye on their vacation to a health farm in Mexico.

Vince was accompanied to Mexico by his favorite girlfriend, Sherry Nelson, who by now had become his Girl Friday, working closely with Vince. as his secretary and confidante.

Significantly, Vince had surrounded himself by now with people who formed a closely knit family.

Besides Sam and Bettye, there was Benny Goldberg.

There was Sherry Nelson.

And there was also Nick Dennis, the little character with the big black mustache who plays Nick Kanavaras, the orderly with the appla and strumberry pie dialect. Vince had known Nick many years in Hollywood; he had played in nearly a score of movies which called for a Greek accent. Nick, a native of Thessaly, once ran a restaurant in New York, the Peerless, on West Forty-Fifth Street. A Greek restaurant, of course.

But today his heart is in Hollywood, his loyalty to Vince.

A happily married man with children, Nick has been perhaps as strong an influence as Bettye and Sam in selling Vince Edwards on the merits and advantages of the institution called marriage.

With Sam and Bettye and Nick and his wife, Mary, all trying to convince Vince that he should settle down, the marriage rumors began trailing Vince and Sherry wherever they went. But sometimes the gossip mill churned up hints of an Edwards romance with other pretty girls.

Sometimes the approach was quaint, such as this *Associated Press* dispatch reporting the trip to Mexico:

"Scandal-mongering is not a worthy occupation but it certainly should be reported that Dr. David Zorba, Ben Casey's chief at County General Hospital, and Dr. Maggie Graham, hospital anesthesiologist and Ben's number-one heart interest, are spending their vacation together. And not bothering to conceal it, what's more.

"This is not grist for the gossip mills, although it does startle *Ben Casey* fans. The two performers, Sam Jaffe and Bettye Ackerman, have been married almost six years . . ."

To this day, many fans don't realize that Bettye Ackerman is Mrs. Sam Jaffe in real life, and think she's in love with Vince Edwards. They tend to confuse Maggie Graham and Ben Casey with the people who play those parts.

Does it disturb Jaffe or Miss Ackerman?

"Not in the least," says Sam. "It's exactly what we want the fans to think. We see it as part of the illusion we have created and want to keep alive."

Some fans who are aware of the matrimonial facts that Sam and Bettye are husband and wife off camera, still won't settle for the explanation that Vince and Bettye are merely play-acting in their *Ben Casey* love sequences. They want to know what gives between the lady doctor and Ben Casey behind the scenes. They won't believe Bettye is a loyal and devoted wife to Sam, and that she's not in the least interested in Vince Edwards—except as a friend and coworker.

"They're cut from the same cloth as the clique which still holds to the concept that the world is flat," laughs Jaffe when the subject comes up. It doesn't disturb him the least that the rumor mongers have a field day building up a nonexistent romance between his wife and the handsome star of their show.

Such disturbances, if they can be called that, are overwhelmingly outweighed by the common interests and common goals held by Vince and by Sam, who at sixty-five is almost twice as old as Vince and certainly old enough to be his father. Nevertheless, the two men conduct themselves as though their age disparity is non-existent.

Aside from their personal similarities, Sam and Vince have many common interests, particularly food. From way back, Sam has been strictly a vegetarian. His wife is a "non-meatarian" also for reasons she'll explain in her own words, later on.

We know from Vince's childhood how he became a strict "organic-food" man, a habit that persists to this day.

Food was one of the factors that drew Sam and Vince closer. It happened after they became acquainted on the set. Vince asked Sam how he met Bettye.

"In a health-food shop," Sam replied straightfaced, which led to mutual revelations about their eating habits.

Sam told Vince why he steers clear of meat.

"When I was a kid on the East Side," he said, "I went to a farm one summer and saw a calf butchered. I never wanted to eat meat after that."

Vince then told Sam about himself and his own insistence for food that has been grown without the aid of chemicals and artificial fertilizers, and how he prompted his mother to shop in specialty stores that carried only organically grown foods.

His strong feelings for Vince have often carried Sam to the precipice of heated argument with some detractors and critics who find fault with the star's outbursts of temperament on the set.

One day someone came up to Jaffe after Edwards blew up during a reading and complained, "Your boy, Vince, is all nerves. Is he trying to play the angry young man in real life, too?"

Sam looked the man squarely in the eye, burning with anger. But he held his temper back and managed to mutter a reply with quiet dignity.

"Have you any conception of what it means to learn the equivalent of three-fifths of a Broadway play every single week?" Jaffe asked. "That's what Vince has to do, to carry the burden of this show. Just picture the strain on him. Why, there isn't an actor alive who could keep on doing this and not show the tension."

Ben Casey has drawn Vincent Edwards and Sam Jaffe together into a bond of friendship that is a rarity in the hectic whirlpool of television life, where tensions and troubles between co-stars are as commonplace as sand on the Sahara.

And there can be no higher tribute to an actor than when Sam Jaffe speaks about Vince Edwards and says in his very finest Dr. Zorba tone—

"Such a boy!"

13
DR. MAGGIE GRAHAM EXAMINES DR. CASEY
(BETTYE ACKERMAN ON VINCE EDWARDS)

BECAUSE SHE is a woman, Bettye Ackerman can cry easily. She cries easily in *Ben Casey* but the fans seldom see the tears. They don't always show on the TV screen because the takes are discarded on the cutting room floor. Sometimes, however, Bettye will be seen in a weepy sequence, but even then it's not precisely what the script has called for. But the director leaves the scene alone—it's more than he bargained for, and better than he'd expected.

Take the time in one *Ben Casey* episode when an alcoholic was admitted to the County Hospital for the thirteenth time after failing to break the habit. Something about the scene moved Bettye deeply. She actually broke down and cried—and it wasn't called for in the scene. It was left in.

"I managed to steal the spotlight from those two giants in my TV life," Bettye says. The giants she spoke of were Dr. Casey and Dr. Zorba who, by Bettye's own admission, make her hope and pray she won't get "lost" in the scenes she plays with them.

233

"They're simply overpowering," she complains with sweet understanding.

There was another time that Bettye broke up unexpectedly and they printed that tearful episode, too. It was the time when Cliff Robertson appeared in the *Ben Casey* series as a guest star.

There'd been a great deal of joking before the scene filmed. A visitor to the set remarked to Vince that Cliff looked quite healthy for a patient who was scripted to die in the next scene.

"Oh," cracked Vince, waving his scalpel, "he won't be so healthy when I'm through with him in surgery."

Then when Robertson died in the next segment, Bettye—or Dr. Maggie Graham—was so over-wrought by the situation that she burst into fitful sobbing.

Some weeks. later, after that particular show appeared on TV, Bettye was informed that the American Medical Association had filed a protest over that scene.

"Doctors, female or otherwise," the AMA advised, "do not get so emotionally involved with their patients."

Bettye hurried to tell Sam Jaffe about the AMA complaint, and was ready to weep on her husband's shoulder. She would have, too, if Sam hadn't chuckled.

"Why are you laughing?" Bettye asked.

"Maybe next time you won't get so smart, young lady, and try to steal the scene with your tears," replied Sam good-naturedly.

Bettye loves the role of Maggie Graham in *Ben Casey*. She has never enjoyed a part more. When she wrote her views about the role of Maggie not long ago for *TV Radio Mirror Magazine*, Bettye gave an intimate glimpse of the character she portrays.

"She's uncomplicated, really," Bettye said. "She's an intelligent, sympathetic person, competent as a professional but feminine to the core. Most of all, I like the subtle relationship that hovers between her and Dr. Casey.

"There is a hint of something more than affection, a trace of romance like faint perfume in the air. And yet it never intrudes on their friendly, medical cooperation and their ardent dedications to the saving of lives.

"Always, without preaching, a delicate message is put forth to the effect that, however they may secretly feel toward each other, it's all sublimated to the demands of their profession."

Bettye's own background is far removed from those two New Yorkers who hover over her in every scene. Bettye was born in Cottageville, South Carolina, on February 29, a leap-year baby. Her early life was real "small-towny," as she calls it. She went to Columbia College in South Carolina, studied drama with Mary Lou Kramer, then switched to Columbia University in New York where she studied pantomime and dance with Louise Gifford.

"Drama and dancing were my passions," she says. She continued studies with Carola Goya, and drama with Alexander Kirklaand at the Theater Wing and in the studios of Stella Adler and Herbert Berghof.

After five seasons of summer stock, commercials on radio and TV, Bettye could afford to try her hand in off-Broadway stuff. That's the starvation circuit.

One of the plays was Moliere's *Tartuffe*—which starred none other than the incomparable Sam Jaffe.

"When I looked at him in those days," says Bettye, "all I could see, alas, was *Gunga Din*. It was the one film I had seen him in, up to then, and I thought he was not only a masterly performer but the cutest thing in that little didie."

Six months later, Bettye Ackerman became Mrs. Sam Jaffe. The marriage got off to a profitable venture right from the outset. Sam and Bettye were taken on by a national touring company of *The Lark*, which starred Julie Harris.

"Our working honeymoon took us around the world and lasted three wonderful years," Bettye relates.

In June, 1962, just when the first year's production on *Ben Casey* came to a conclusion, Bettye and Sam celebrated their sixth wedding anniversary.

Bettye and Sam have enjoyed a successful marriage despite the wide difference in their ages because, among many reasons, they see eye-to-eye on many matters. Food is one of the subjects they agree on wholeheartedly.

As mentioned previously, Sam is a vegetarian, Bettye a "non-meatarian." It cooks down to the time when Bettye was eight. Suddenly one day her pet duck, Waddle, disappeared. At dinner, Bettye stared in abject horror at the sumptuous dish her mother had prepared.

"Waddle!" Bettye screamed and ran to her room in tears. Her brother did the same.

"To this day," Bettye says, "my poor mother apologizes for having cooked Waddle. She hadn't realized that we'd been making a pet of the duck while she was fatting him for the kill."

So, Bettye's reason for not eating meat is perhaps as sentimental as Sam's, which was an outgrowth of seeing a calf slaughtered before his eyes. But beyond that, Sam and Bettye believe that the vegetable way is the only way to good and prolonged health. Their queasiness about meat dinners has subsided through the years. Now they'll serve guests meat—even fowl—at home dinners. But Bettye and Sam will never touch it themselves.

Beyond the enjoyment Bettye receives from her part of Maggie Graham, she also gains satisfaction. That comes when she receives letters from fans who praise her for her heroic woman's role in the world of medicine. One letter that Bettye prizes over the others came from a girl who was prompted to enter the medical profession—after watching *Ben Casey*.

"I want to be an anesthesiologist like Dr. Maggie and I'd like to be that fine a human being," the girl wrote.

"As an actress," Bettye remarked, "I'm flattered that she was influenced by the character I portray."

Bettye and Sam are extremely happy in their work. Bettye is as tolerant of Vince Edwards' occasional temperamental outbursts as Sam is. She seems to understand why the young man with the angry profile is constantly on edge, ready to jump down a director's throat or cut up a fuss over some inconvenience, real or imagined.

"I see him as a man who is very much like my Sam, except that Vince is finding difficulty in achieving the tranquil pleasures that Sam and I glory in—enjoying life, nature, and people as we make our small contributions in enriching the lives of others.

"Sam will always defend Vince against the people who complain about his anger and temperament. I agree with Sam's view that Vince is carrying the show on his shoulders and that the work is back-breaking.

"Sam is right. Absolutely. Vince is in three-fifths of each segment of the series. It's a wonder he hasn't lost his sense of humor entirely. He has a very keen one."

We haven't cited many instances of Vince's humor thus far, so here's a case which can stand as proof positive that he does enjoy an occasional laugh.

A woman tourist visited the set one day during rehearsal and spotted Vince's stand-in, Ray Joyer. The woman rushed up and fussed wildly over him. One moment she called him "Vince Casey" and the next "Dr. Edwards." It was the nearest exhibition of delirium that the *Ben Casey* set had seen.

The poor stand-in was helpless. He tried to explain that the real Dr. Ben Casey was the bloke standing beside him, the bloke who was breaking up with laughter at the comical situation. But the woman wouldn't hear Ray out.

After she left, Ray exploded.

"Why the hell didn't you tell her who you were?" he demanded.

Vince kept laughing.

"She was happy with you, wasn't she?" he replied. "That's all that really counts."

Bettye views this incident as a mark of the man they call Ben Casey.

"Although he is weighed down with so many responsibilities," Bettye says in all earnestness, "Vince retains a large tolerance and ability to smile charitably at the foibles of human beings.

"I think in time he will settle down and sail in calmer waters. Perhaps marriage will do that for Vince."

Vince himself tends to agree with Bettye's philosophy.

"I'm a bachelor who has urges, now and then, to make the big jump into matrimony," says Vince. "Somehow, I always shied away when I got near the starting gate. But lately, working with Sam and Bettye, I've been getting a change of heart.

"Those two make marriage seem like the best chance for happiness in this troubled world. It's easy to see they love each other and—what's more important—their love seems to spill over and touch everyone who's near them.

"I admire them both, greatly. They are a well-read, much-traveled, and very cultured lady and gentleman of show business. I've never heard an unkind word leave their mouths. Each is exceptionally cooperative on the set. Their main concern is for the cast and crew, for the success of the show. Maybe when you're that happy, you stop thinking about yourself.

"What more can I say? I guess it's clear that I respect, admire, and am extremely fond of these two fine people."

14
VINCE EDWARDS EXAMINES DR. CASEY

"THE ANTICIPATION of success was far greater than the reality. I've found that success is really a pain in the posterior so far as my personal life goes. . ."

Vince Edwards pulls no punches. He talks straight from his beamy shoulder. He savors the success and security that have come to him as the hottest new star of videoland. But he resents some of the marathon trials and annoyances that pepper him like a shower of asteroids from day to day as he whirls through his orbit of stardom.

"It's always 'do this' or 'do that' or 'come here,' " he says, complaining about the loss of his personal life to fame. "It's a price a successful actor must pay, but it's a big price. I often wonder if it's worth it.

"I find it hardest to adjust to the attitude of friends. They treat me differently—they back off and seem all at once to believe the publicity they've read about me. Old friends suddenly get nervous talking with me.

"It's the illusion of being a star—and I don't like it."

Vince is quick to admit this is what he wanted. He never had second thoughts about deprivations he would have to endure once he became a star. He believed the road would be combed with milk and honey.

"Certainly I derive pleasure from it," Vince admits.

"Certainly I have financial security, which is what I've always wanted," he also admits.

"But," he adds with Woe in his tone, "I've won a kind of pyrrhic victory."

On the plus side, Vince can point to the pleasure he gets from seeing producers and directors who turned him down for years suddenly ringing him up, asking him to work for them.

"It's gratifying to listen to their offers," he says "Two years ago they wouldn't let me past the door to see their secretaries. Now they call me up and want me in their homes to talk over ideas for movies."

But Vince can't simply leap at the first good offer that comes along, whether it's from a movie figure who wouldn't give Vince the right time in the past, or a film tycoon with whom Edwards had no prior dealings.

"I'm no longer an individual," Vince points out with measured pangs of regret. "I've become a corporation. I refer to myself now as 'We.' I can't do anything alone anymore—there are agents and lawyers and managers and other people who've got to have a voice in everything I do."

Vince also feels the pressures of playing *Ben Casey* day in and day out, week after week.

"It's gotten so bad with all the medical terminology I've got to learn that I hardly have time to go on a date, let alone get married.

"When I go to bed at night, I have to take Merck with me."

hat's the medical dictionary.

Vince exudes an iron-jawed disdain for things that displease him, which is part of his nature. For that reason, perhaps, Vince is able to play the saturnine neurosurgeon who bullies patients and colleagues alike week after week with the same overbearing satisfaction.

This sustained disdain for things that displease him has reached out increasingly of late, as evidenced by the criticism Vince has generated for his new way of life. But Vince has enough wisdom to realize that all the disturbing influences are part of the way of life he chose.

It's simply the freightage he's got to pay on the highway of glory he travels.

Yet he feels it was all too long in coming.

"I'm a twelve-year overnight success," he says repeatedly when reminded that he rocketed to stardom after one churlish performance in the hour of incision.

Trying to analyze his popularity, Vince reasons:

"America wants a father image. Like Billy Graham. They're fanatics. And there's no cure for this."

He gets a kick, however, out of hearing how endearingly the medical profession has taken to his program—and him. Hospitals from Maine to California report incidents that form the great national discussion over his rugged bedside manner.

In a Midwestern hospital, *Look* magazine reported recently, a delirious woman patient started yelling for Dr. Ben Casey. Her own doctor, a mild-mannered medico, finally quieted her by pulling a Casey—he screamed at the nurses!

The success of Dr. Casey's coast-to-coast practice is in evidence in hospitals everywhere. In New York City's St. Vincent's Hospital, the nurses were given special dispensation to stay up until 11 P.M. before lights out so they could watch the Casey brand of medical reality.

Doctors themselves stay up to watch and some even go so far as to talk over cases with Casey.

"It's true," Vince said, "since I've been playing this role, ministers, little old ladies, everybody—

even doctors—discuss cases with me. It's medical madness."

But Vince has tired considerably of the endless medical gags that have sprouted like bedsores from his residency at the same old operating stand every week.

"I don't mind it fifty or sixty times a day," Edwards says with dismay, "but when it gets to be eighty or more, it's downright monotonous. It's gotten so bad I don't dare get sick lest I end up in the hospital myself as a patient. When I had the flu, I wanted to go to the hospital, but I wouldn't chance it. Nobody would have believed it was for real and not a gag."

Vince is chided a great deal about his acting and his mannerisms, especially the irresistability he displays for standing constantly with arms folded. It got so that *New York Times* critic Jack Gould suggested that Dr. Casey "has exhausted all conceivable methods of folding his arms."

"What do they want me to do," Vince asks, "cut them off?"

One woman, the wife of a resident in internal medicine in a Pennsylvania hospital, suggested a solution to help Dr. Casey break the habit. She said hospital laundries are notorious for the large amount of starch used in washing. Her husband and his colleagues, she reported, always have to exert great force in separating and opening jacket sleeves, trouser legs, and pockets when they're getting into their uniforms.

"Perhaps the hospital in which Ben emotes provides this same service," she said. "If so, then it is probable that Ben has to keep his arms folded for it may be impossible for him to get his hands into his pockets.

"One solution, which my husband has found effective, to take a pair of ordinary household pliers—and *tug!*"

Vince regards this lady's suggestion and all the thousands of others that have poured in, offering advice on aspects of his acting, as part of the audience's vast sense of identification with the medical situations being dramatized.

"That's the way it is," Vince cracked. 'Tm a doctor with thirty-two million patients. If people write to me and tell me how they'd like me to be, I don't take exception to their gestures. It goes to prove that we are doing an effective job—the viewers are projecting themselves into the situations, and the show becomes a matter of personal interest and concern to them.

"It's a good thing that I don't take some of the suggestions seriously. If I did I'd lose my sanity."

One of the prize letters Vince received came from a woman from Massachusetts who wrote to

"Dr. Ben Casey, Hollywood." True to his repute in such matters, the postman delivered the letter.

"Dear Dr. Casey," it began. "I am going into the hospital next week for an operation, but I don't want my doctor to perform the surgery. That's why I'm writing to you. I would appreciate it very much if you could take my case. I know you are a neuro-surgeon, so I can't ask you to do the operation—I must have my gall bladder removed. However, I'd like you to be a consultant on the case.

"I'd like Dr. Maggie Graham to administer the anesthesia, Dr. Zorba to do the surgery, and Dr. Gillespie to put in the stitches. Afterward, I would like Dr. Kildare to care for me during my convalescence.

"Can you please let me know if this can be arranged. Please let me know soonest because the pain from my gall bladder is killing me."

This letter indubitably points up with startling reality the impact medical dramas have had on some people. Whether the letter writer was a kibitzer or some kind of a nut, we'll never know. Needless to say, no one but a Rockefeller or a millionaire with comparable status could afford to have all the medical talent demanded by this woman at her bedside.

Which all goes to prove that Vince Edwards is riding the crest of a video vogue that is here to stay a while.

And he wants to leave it?

Why I'll never know, nor will the millions of fans who now live more placid lives since *Ben Casey* came on the air like a potent sedative and relieved the interminable suffering endured by the public that had been exposed to the nerve-jangling whodunits and explosive sagebrush horse operas.

As the 1962-'63 season came into its own, one could almost feel the comforting metamorphosis. Quiet hospital scenes replaced the hellfire and brimstone of the six-shooter dramas.

The only shots heard out West these days are those being fired by the cowboys at themselves— committing suicide because they didn't go through medical school.

15
THE FUTURE

THERE IS NO imminent danger that Vincent Edwards will become a hardship case and fall back into the dismal days when he was a struggling, unsuccessful thespian stubbing his toe on the impregnable outer defenses of stardom.

Through Vince Edwards' personality, *Ben Casey* has become one of videoland's top shows and it looks good for a long run. But Vince isn't keen about a long run.

"Two more years," he says. "Then I'll do something else."

What?

"There are movies and there are nightclubs and records. And I can write shows and produce them. The field is wide open to me now—thanks to *Ben Casey*."

No one appreciates the success *Ben Casey* has brought to him more than Vince Edwards. But he doesn't feel he is ungrateful or unappreciative to those who enabled him to reach the pinnacle when he threatens to shed his doctor's jacket and hang up his stethoscope by 1965.

Ask Vince why he wants to give up a good thing and his answer is generally always the same.

"I won't do a series for more than three years. I don't want saturation. Three seasons means nearly three years out of my life. It's too tough a job. I want to enjoy my life. I don't want to blow my health either."

Vince eyes the future confidently.

"There's a lot ahead for me. I want to have a say in things. If an actor doesn't become a producer, who will? The plumber? Look at some of the actors who've made it—Dick Powell, Kirk Douglas, Burt Lancaster, Sheldon Reynolds. I can go on and on.

"There's a great future and I've got to take advantage of it soon before I lose the opportunity."

Vince mentions recordings. His baritone voice is good. When he cut "Widgit" and "Lollipop," Vince had had little opportunity to rehearse and prepare for the recording session. Consequently he was "cold" and the discs were surpassed in both quality and sales by the highly professional rendition turned out by The Chordettes.

But after hitting it big with *Ben Casey* Vince turned to voice training again in what little spare time he had. He was better than sensational on the *Dinah Shore Show* and, afterward, gave a great deal of thought to singing. The result was an album, "Ben Casey Sings."

By the end of 1962, it was one of the hottest albums on the market. Among the tunes are such conventional standbys as "Stormy Weather," "As Time Goes By," and "Don't Worry 'Bout Me."

Critics agree that Sinatra has nothing to worry about—but neither does Vince Edwards. His agent, Abby Greshler, is still counting the receipts from the royalties.

Vince claims that the role of neurosurgeon—the doctor image—is forced on him too much off screen. Many people seem to believe Vincent Edwards is a doctor, yet he knows they know he's not.

"They seem to crave an image like Ben Casey," he says. "It's almost a spiritual thing. Television provides symbols—and I happen to be one of them. Even the kids come up and tell me they love Ben Casey. That's a responsibility I have to live up to. I'm forced to do the best I can as an actor and as a person. In private life, I behave with abstract goodness."

Consequently, Vince feels the pressure building up. Monotony, too. Perhaps not yet, but in time he'll feel boredom with the role of Ben Casey. Before then, Vince vows he'll bow out and try other things.

In the days of old, Hollywood brought stars along on a slow, methodical, well-planned buildup which often took years to complete. Today, the magic of the cathode tube projects an unknown face into thirty million homes and, *voila*—a star is born overnight!

It happened to Vince Edwards and he is quite aware of his good fortune in becoming an instant star.

Not long before he died, Clark Gable told writer Bill Davidson what he thought of the phenomenon of stardom. It was a typically candid observation by one of the screen's great personages.

"I'm, just a lucky slob from Ohio," said Gable. "I happened to be in the right place at the right time, and I had lots of smart guys helping me. Without them I'd probably still be driving a truck somewhere."

When Davidson mentioned this morsel of Gable philosophy to Edwards during an interview, Vince didn't concede that he, too, was a lucky slob from Brooklyn who hit it big in Hollywood.

"That's what's the trouble with this business," he replied. "They don't want actors. They're just waiting for the next truck driver to come along."

There are many television viewers even today who think Vince wouldn't qualify to drive a truck—they prefer to think of him as a guy who should be wearing a black leather jacket and riding on the back of a motorcycle.

Maybe so. And undoubtedly it's true that Vince, who performs miracles with his scalpel every Monday night, can't even operate on a hard-boiled egg.

But when a producer-director like Carl Foreman summons Vince Edwards to London for a command performance with such co-stars as Peppard and Hamilton and Schiaffino—the future must be bright for the surly surgeon.

Perhaps Vince's dreams of becoming a great motion picture star, a great director, a great producer will come true. Perhaps not.

But as he cuts his swath across the firmament of our time, Vince Edwards accommodates all the promise of achieving the greatness and lofty goals to which he aspires.

If he doesn't accomplish all those, then perhaps he may settle on being just another Clark Gable.

THE END

Made in United States
Orlando, FL
05 December 2024

55050497R00150